Mary,
Queen of Scots

MADELEINE
BINGHAM

(Mansell Collection)

Mary,

Queen of Scots

by

Madeleine Bingham

INTERNATIONAL
PROFILES

Mary, Queen of Scots
© Madeleine Bingham, 1969

ISBN 0.249.44011.3

INTERNATIONAL PROFILES

General Editor: EDWARD STORER

Published by:
International Textbook Company Limited
158 Buckingham Palace Road, London, S.W.1

Series Design: Melvyn Gill   *Pictorial Research:* F. G. Thomas
Colour Plates: Photoprint Plates Limited, Wickford, Essex
Covers: George Over Limited, London and Rugby
Paper: Frank Grunfeld (Sales) Limited, London
Text and Binding: Butler and Tanner Limited, London and Frome

Introduction

1. *Mary, Queen of Scots, from the lead medal by Jacopo Primavera c. 1572 (British Museum)*

Those who die well attract the courtesies of history. The manner and heroism of their death can obliterate the folly of their policies and the ambiguity of their characters.

Mary, Queen of Scots is of this company.

To read about her is to see numerous reflections in mirrors. Some shadow the martyr dying for the old religion. Others sharply and prismatically show the adulteress of Protestant invective. Yet others depict the romantic shadow of the wronged Queen, in the toils of that astute Renaissance Prince, Queen Elizabeth of England.

Over the centuries, the Queen of Scots has become a catalyst. According to the tenets of their beliefs the Protestants, the Calvinists, and the Catholics have used her to reinforce their theories, their distortions of history, and their slanted views of cruelties practised in the cause of religion.

French historians see her as a French princess caught in the web of the machiavellian Elizabeth and her spider, William Cecil. English historians depict her as a threat to a country terrified of a war on two fronts.

The Scots present a divided picture—she is either a symbol of noble nationalism repressed by England, or a Queen, lustful, yet intent on forcing a discredited Catholicism on an unwilling and newly purged Puritan country.

It is difficult for later generations to understand the fanaticism of religious wars, or, in an age when the decay of any form of religion is regarded as normal, to appreciate the outrage felt by Catholics when a Protestant cleric pronounced a long sermon to a Queen about to die steadfastly true to her Catholic faith. It is equally hard to be fair to the furies of John Knox intent on purging the abuses of the old Church.

The tragedy of Mary Stuart is overlaid with propaganda from both sides. Into her grave and beyond she is pursued by conflict. Over the centuries the documents have accumulated, and under the weight of their conflicting evidence it is tempting to place reliance on 'original sources'.

But even these are clouded with distortions. An English ambassador to France might well write the truth to Elizabeth, and to William Cecil. On the other hand he was dependent on their favours. It could be that, like any messenger to a great prince, he would temper his evidence to please the ears of his hearers. In the sixteenth century the stakes were high. People in a century which believed in heaven and hell were not slow to give their enemies the chance to find out in which direction their fate had led them.

Even if the letters of Mary Stuart and Queen Elizabeth are used as evidence, belief can be suspended. How far was Elizabeth disingenuous in her protestations of friendship to her 'dear sister', or how far was the 'dear sister' trying to deceive Elizabeth in her equally fervent protestations of good faith and amity?

Words are often the cloak of deeds, not a statement of good faith, and the people of the Renaissance were masters of words. In their literature a glittering array of words dazzles the mind, while the eye recoils from the bloody deeds which mar the century.

These people lived in danger—of treachery, of spies, of murder, of the axe, of hanging, drawing and quartering. Against the elegant sound of lutes, and the rustle of skirts across the crushed thyme walks, must be set the executioner's hand plucking a heart from a living body.

It was not a century to be on the losing side.

On to the centre of this stage walked Mary Stuart, a beautiful woman, clever, well-read, elegantly educated, with a facility for verse, a sweet voice, a neat hand at embroidery, great physical courage, and above all— charm.

Even her enemies admitted her charm. Right to the end, when the axe fell, she exercised her charm and could inspire devotion in those who surrounded her.

What is charm? It is an indefinable characteristic, like a morning mist, hard to recapture.

While Elizabeth's voice rings back over the centuries, with clear precision, the voice of Mary is muted, overlaid with her charm. Everything about her seems to be reported by others, while she herself disappears into the mists of the land of her birth. To read about her is to go à la Recherche de la Reine Perdue.

Even now her charm, like the aroma which arises from opening an old perfume bottle, has the power to arouse passion and partisans as it did in her lifetime.

Who was she?

2. *Mary, Queen of Scots* (Scottish National Portrait Gallery)

Chapter I

3. *James V* (*Scottish National Portrait Gallery*)

It was the destiny of Mary, Queen of Scots to be an apple of discord from the moment of her birth.

To her sick father, James V, the fact of her sex was the last blow in a series of defeats. His armies were in flight, his two infant sons dead, and his realm riven by the clash of the clans.

His crown had become a burden too heavy to be borne. When he was told his wife had given birth to a girl, his weary words: 'The de'il go with it, it will end as it began, it came with a lass, and it will pass with a lass' were in a sense prophetic, for James VI became James I of England.

Mary Stuart was born at Linlithgow on the 8 December 1542. Like the winter skies of Scotland under which she was born, her inheritance was grey. Her father died five days later, of a compound of sickness, grief, and disappointment. At least he died in his bed. Mary's other Scottish an-

cestors had all died bloodily, either battling against the English, or treacherously, at the hands of their own nobles.

Her mother, Marie de Guise Lorraine of France, the second wife of James V, had both the intelligence and the ambition of the Guise family, but whether from choice or from weariness she did not exert her Regency to the full. Like her daughter, she fell under the uncertain sway of Scottish factions.

While Marie de Guise was still in childbed, James Hamilton, Earl of Arran, was at her side proposing to marry his eldest son to the newborn child. Arran had some claims to the Scottish throne. He was trying to consolidate them.

But before the child had opened her eyes on her future kingdom other marriage projects hung over her cradle. Henry VIII was already in the matrimonial field, proposing his son Edward VI as her future husband. Henry's sister, Margaret Tudor, had been married to James IV of

Scotland. Her flight into England with a mere earl, after the death of her husband at Flodden, was unfortunate. But the whims of women could not be allowed to spoil a political project. The Union of England and Scotland was a project, a dream. The sex of the child could be turned to political advantage. Henry VIII was returning to the sensible policy of his father.

Like many sixteenth-century proposals, the idea was simple, but the execution devious. It was interlaced with Scotsmen in the pay of the English king, considered as traitors by their own countrymen, and secret clauses which guaranteed the Scottish succession to Henry VIII and his heirs, should the unfortunate demise of the infant Mary occur.

Rumours were rife. The cautious Scots suspected, perhaps with reason, that if the infant Queen were in the care of her relative, Henry VIII, she might not survive. The King, on the other hand, suspected—perhaps with even more reason—that she might be spirited away into the dubious care of François I of France. For there were other Scots who saw the throne of France as a glittering prize for the infant Queen, and a way of enlarging their own political power. The children of kings, like modern block votes, were pawns in a long-term political game.

In the event, the Scots defied Henry's pretensions to the Scottish throne by crowning Mary as Queen of the Scots at Stirling, on the 9 September 1543. She was nine months old. To the quick-tempered Henry this was a challenge to be met without delay. He despatched a herald to declare war on Scotland unless the infant Queen was delivered to him.

The Scots, equally sensitive, then declared all their countrymen who had been negotiating with Henry to be traitors. They began seriously to turn their attention to France as a potentially more useful ally, since Marie de Guise was the mother of their Queen. Henry's forthright answer to this was to invade Scotland and lay Edinburgh to waste.

The death of Henry VIII did not allay the march of the fates towards the child Mary. Protector Somerset still demanded that Mary, envisaged as the future wife of Edward VI, should be handed over to the English. This new demand strengthened the hand of Mary's mother in her own determination to turn to the French for help. And Henri II, now King of France, was ready with reassurances.

This renewed challenge had its inevitable result: again the English invaded Scotland. At the battle of Pinkie Cleugh ten thousand Scots fell on the field. Scotland was now wide open to the English.

But the prize of battle, Mary, had eluded them.

The first of Mary's hurried journeys and escapes had taken place. At night, in the greatest secrecy, the child was taken first to Stirling, and then to Inchmahome. It was a secret, remote place, and to reach it the child made her first journey by water, to the island abbey in the lake, surrounded by the mists of her dark kingdom. Even today it is a quiet, remote place where the ruined archways frame distant views of trees and water.

Ronsard called Scotland a barbarous country and a brutal people, but here, in the depths of the 'barbarous country', the child was safe in the care of the monks, protected by the distance and the silence.

It was here, too, that the 'four Maries' of the old poem joined her as playmates. They were Mary Fleming, Mary Beaton, Mary Livingstone, and Mary Seton. Their stay at the abbey was not to be long. The wind of politics was soon blowing their way again.

The Estates met. Under the lash of English arms, it now seemed a good moment indeed for the Scots to revive the 'auld alliance' with France which the Queen Regent had been urging. The child was their only ace, and they decided to play her. They betrothed the child Queen to the French Dauphin.

In July 1548, accompanied by her four Maries, the Queen of the Scots left her kingdom for France, and the child King Edward VI lost the bride he had never seen.

The spectacle of the five innocent children, the five Maries, on the French warship, rosy and smiling, running about amongst the tough sailors is a picture which attracts romantic historians. Some describe the little girls examining the guns, others somehow appear to know that only Mary Stuart did not feel seasick.

Children are strange and logical creatures, not slow to sense the undercurrents of feeling in the adults who surround them. They accept the exigencies of their fate more easily than adults. The child Mary was probably quite aware of the pomp and circumstance of her departure, of her own importance as she walked from the Castle over the drawbridge to the waiting ship.

It is for this reason, the influences of early childhood, that it is important, in seeking clues to the ingredients in Mary Stuart's character, to stress the conditions of her earlier childhood years, and in particular her transition from the austerities of Scotland to the luxury of the French Court.

The ship, evading the waiting English, arrived safely at Roscoff in Brittany. The escape was providential and fatal. Mary was five years and eight months old when she left her 'barbarous country', riven by feuds, for the softer land of France.

About this voyage, Knox said that it was 'to the end that in her youth, Mary should drink of the liquor that should remain with her all her lifetime for a plague to her realm, and for her final destruction'.

The words may well have been conceived in the bitterness of a man who had served in the French galleys, but they were prophetic. For Mary was half French, and when she left Scotland she left at such an early age that probably few impressions, except perhaps the remembrance of the monks, the hurried journeys, and the escapes, would remain with her. Lost memories persist, and children do not need to be told of the spice of dangers which they feel with their nerves, but do not truly fear because they are excitingly overcome. It was perilous stuff for the mind of a sixteenth-century child, leading, one may think, to the subconscious view that panache and perilous adventures must lead to a happy outcome.

The temporary outcome for Mary was certainly pleasant. The Court of Henri II, the Court of the Valois, was the most brilliant and cultured in Europe. It was well fitted to be the nurturing ground of her latent talents.

Under François I, France had become heir to all the arts of the Italian Renaissance. It was a country in which they were to take root and flourish. Architects came to turn the valley of the Loire into a country of palaces. Painters, sculptors, and decorators transformed the French chateaux into jewels. Colleges were founded, and François' sister, Marguerite of Angoulême, an amiable and learned princess, fostered the arts, and defended artists against persecution and intolerance. In that Court, it was said, 'the courtiers were learned, and the learned were courtiers'.

The courts under both François I and Henri II were glittering stages on which a continual feast for all the senses was unrolled. They were also backdrops for what is known as 'galanterie', a euphemistic cover for charming words and pretty speeches, or plain licence. Among the poets and the painters drifted the ladies of beauty and questionable virtue.

But while some French chroniclers stress the brilliance of the French Court, others lay emphasis on its corruption. Henri II passed on his syphilitic blood to Mary's future husband. The 'galanterie' had its disadvantages.

It was also a society in which a royal mistress, Diane de Poitiers, could win and keep the favours of the King. The stakes were not low.

The Château of Chambord is, to this day, a monument to the ladies of these courts. Set in its great park where the stag hunts took place, the ground floor is simple, while the roof is intricately decorated. Here the ladies could drift between the fairy-tale turrets, and flirt, or watch the chase from their high vantage point. Other, and less strenuous, chases certainly took place in the embrasures between the elaborate stone carvings. Into this court, of learning and licence, Mary arrived in the summer of 1548.

To the opening senses of the child these troupes of beautiful women, gallant men, grand princes, and high dignitaries of the Church, must have seemed as an array of peacocks to set against the dun-coloured grouse of her Scottish background. Yet these people were her blood relations. She was, and doubtless grew aware of it, the cherished child of their expectations and their ambitions.

Although Mary had been especially recommended to the care of her grandmother, Antoinette de Bourbon, Duchesse de Guise, it was decided that in view of her future prospects, and to assure her uncles' ambitions for her, she should be brought up at St Germain-en-Laye with the other royal children, François, the Dauphin, destined to be her future husband,

and his sisters, Elizabeth, Claude, and Marguerite, three small girls who became Queen of Spain, Duchess of Lorraine, and Queen of Navarre.

These children were to be well grounded in the arts and all forms of learning. French education, even in those days, was a hard school. Elegance of phrasing and moral maxims were dinned into them. These themes from improving books were re-worked into the form of letters, presumably to fix both the sentiments and the style into the minds of the children. Some of Mary's essays in the form of letters to her sisters-in-law, particularly to Elizabeth de Valois, have survived.

> The true greatness and excellence of a Prince, my beloved sister, is not in dignity, in gold, in jewels, and other pomps of fortune, but in prudence, in virtue, in wisdom, and in knowledge. And as much as a Prince wishes to be different from his people in habit and in his way of life, so much more must he be separated from the stupid opinions of the vulgar. Farewell, and love me as much as you can.

This was a lesson which must have been well conned by the little princess. But although she may have ostensibly disdained the pomps and ephemeral nature of the outward show of princes, though she was always to remain aware of that dignity of the princess which separated her from the ordinary everyday opinions and actions of 'the vulgar', prudence and true wisdom were two of the recommendations of the maxim which she was never to learn. Mary Stuart showed a great aptitude as a scholar, which delighted her teachers and relations. She learned Italian very quickly, and spoke it as well as she spoke French. But French was to remain her mother tongue. It was her way of understanding and expressing herself from the age of six and for the rest of her life. The French language conditioned her way of thinking, and was the ocean in which her thoughts swam.

Like Queen Elizabeth, Mary learned Greek and Latin. These were the new accomplishments for the learned ladies of the Renaissance. Although she never made any great inroads into the intricacies of Greek, at the age of thirteen she was able to give a discourse in Latin, at the New Year's festivities, in the Great Hall of the Louvre before the King and Queen. This discourse, which astonished the Court, was dedicated to the proposition that 'it is suitable for women to study all forms of learning and the liberal arts'.

The chronicler Brantôme speaks about Mary's discourse in tones of astonishment and awe: 'Think what a wonderful and admirable sight it was to see this beautiful and learned Queen, thus discoursing in Latin which she understood and spoke well.' And then, as if to refute disbelief, he adds: 'I know, because I saw her there.'

This dedicated and well-behaved pupil also learned geography and history, and it was generally accepted at Court that the young Queen had exceptional gifts, a rare imagination, and a great love and understanding of poetry. In poetry her preceptor was Ronsard, and it was he who directed her first steps towards facility in verse. She was not only learned for a child, but she had an agreeable singing voice and accompanied herself on the lute.

But there the threads of her mixed ancestry divide. On the one side is the picture of the 'princesse lointaine', singing at her lute, poring over her books, or bent over her embroidery with delicate fingers. On the other side is the Scot who loved hunting and hawking, and followed the chase with dash, ardour, and courage. The fierce, brave strain of the border raiders, her Scottish ancestors, was still apparent. This was the warp of the web she wove of her conflicting traits.

Above all, her beauty made her the centre of attention at the Court of Henri II. Ronsard hymned her praises:

> At the spring's centre, amongst the lilies,
> Her body shimmered whiter than the lilies, and fairer,
> And the roses, stained with the blood of Adonis,
> Were by her soft cheeks drained of colour.

Du Bellay, another poet of the Court, says: 'Be content, my eyes, you will never see anything more fair.'

Yet even her beauty has an ambiguous quality about it. Her hair is variously described as chestnut, fair, and brown, or even black. In portraits her eyes seem dark brown or black, and in some pictures the young Queen looks plain, and it is difficult to believe in the hymned beauty. It must have been a mobile face which was lit with animation and charm.

But a young lady who is brought up surrounded by such universal praise and admiration would be less than human if she were not to believe some part of it. She would accept that she was clever, beautiful, and accomplished; in addition, she would know that she was being trained to walk through this glittering Court as its first and noblest ornament.

Already a Queen, she could be forgiven for thinking that she was destined to be a greater Queen.

Chapter II

5. *Charles de Lorraine, Cardinal* (Mansell Collection)

If the poets of the French Court hymned Mary's beauty, her relations were no less fulsome in their praise of her other attributes. And although the fact that she was the destined bride of the Dauphin could hardly have worked to her disadvantage, there seems no doubt about the spontaneous and genuine nature of the admiration she aroused. Catherine de Médicis, in the springtime of her pleasure with Mary, wrote to the Queen Regent of Scotland:

> It is impossible to possess more beauty, intelligence, and goodness, than your daughter; in truth she has more of these qualities than could be asked for at her age. She will, I am quite confident, be a blessing and benediction for all those to whom she belongs, and not only for them, but for the whole world. The King is as content with her as you could wish. As for myself, even if I could wish anything at all for her, I would change nothing.

When the child Mary had been at the Court for some time, Catherine still wrote ecstatically: 'I cannot refrain from telling you how marvellously it must add to your felicity to have a daughter such as yours, so beautiful, so good, and excelling in every respect; for my own part, God has been pleased to enrich my portion with real happiness, and to give me a great consolation for my declining years.' This was Mary in her growing years, a paragon.

She had her four playmates, her four Maries, whom she had brought from Scotland, but she was greeted in France by four uncles—of less grace than the Maries, but men of power and vast ambitions.

These were her Guise uncles, the Cardinal of Lorraine, Claude de Guise, François de Guise, and Henri de Guise. For them, and especially for the Cardinal, their niece Mary was a stake in their domination of France and Scotland, and possibly of England itself.

The Cardinal of Lorraine was no less fulsome in his praise. Writing to his sister, the Regent of Scotland, he said: 'Your daughter grows apace, and every day progresses in greatness, goodness, wisdom, and virtue, and is unsurpassed in all things which are virtuous and honest; I must make it known to you, madame, that the King appreciates her so much that he can pass an hour at a time chatting with her.'

Yet by the King's side, in these hours of leisure, there was also his mistress, Diane de Poitiers, Sénéchale of Normandy and Duchesse de Valentinois. Twenty years older than the King, Diane de Poitiers had been thirty-eight when he had fallen under her domination. The Sénéchale wore the royal ermine and jewels. She was queen in all but name, and ruled not only the King but the Court. It was she who directed the education of the King's children.

For, in spite of her outward compliments, the Queen was said not to regard Mary with affection. Possibly the child was as close to the mistress as she was to the King, and the mistress was said to have supervised *la Reinette's* instruction in French manners and deportment. This emphasis on the word 'French' was an implied slur on the Queen, Catherine de Médicis, an Italian.

Nor was Diane de Poitiers the only source of scandal near the growing princess. Her widowed Scottish governess, Lady Fleming, was dismissed from her post for encouraging the attentions of the King. The *maîtresse en titre* did not brook rivals. That the episode was not without foundation was proved by the fact that the governess subsequently bore Henri II a healthy son.

Mary's close connexion to Diane de Poitiers was another thread which was to show its darker side. But it was the springtime of hope, and the Cardinal still wrote that Mary was so good and virtuous that it would not be possible for her to behave better if she had ten governesses. No one, he said, could be more beautiful and honest, or more pious. Yet the words in her praise were backed up by generous deeds. She would write to her mother asking for favours for her entourage—more money for her personal servants, a favour for the son of her old nurse, or maybe a pension for an old retainer. Even as a child she was conscious of the debt she owed to others, and hated to be niggardly.

On one occasion she asked for the gift of an abbey for one of her teachers. 'Not that he requested it, but I have heard it said many times that to serve well deserves well,' she wrote. The teacher for whom Mary requested the abbey was John Erskine—a prior from Inchmahome. Already her thoughtfulness stretched from the present to the past.

While still at the Court of France, many Scots came to pay their respects to her and tender her their allegiance. She was constantly in touch with affairs beyond the sea. Yet by this time she must certainly have been conditioned by her teaching and her environment to see all things from the point of view of France, and of her powerful uncles.

Although she could discourse about politics and the affairs of the world with intelligence and simplicity, it was always to her uncles that she deferred. They were the guiding spirits of her conduct and her ideas. She was the symbol of their continuing power, and they were the guarantee of her ambitions. Their fates were woven together, or so it seemed.

By the time Mary was fifteen, then, she had all the outward accomplishments, and her destiny was ready to be decided. She must now implement the reason for her being brought to France, and marry the King's son.

Unlike Mary, François, the Dauphin, did not earn the plaudits of the courtiers, the ambassadors, or the onlookers from abroad. Contemporary accounts describe him as extraordinarily pale, blown up rather than fat, and more taciturn, and less lively, than most children of his age. He liked weapons and horses, and his passion was for hunting. There was no trace in his character of any inclination towards the arts or any form of learning. He remained always very conscious of his rank, and liked others to render him the outward signs of it.

The picture of the blotchy youth of fourteen set against the fair flower of Scotland with all her accomplishments presents a sombre contrast. Mary and François are described as whispering their little secrets in corners, caressing one another. Would they have been so caressing if they had not known that their mutual fate was already decided?

Meanwhile in December 1557, the Regent of Scotland, Mary's mother, called her parliament together. As a result nine men were to be sent to France to negotiate the contract of marriage. But the delegates were not to consent to the marriage until they had guarantees of the independence of Scotland.

The delegates set sail for France. Their journey was not without incident, for a tempest blew up and sank two of their vessels. Diplomacy had varied dangers in the sixteenth century.

The terms of the contract included a clause in which Mary and François agreed to govern according to the ancient laws of Scotland, and if Mary died then the crown was to pass to the rightful heir. So far so good. Then the actual bargaining began.

The eldest son was to be King of France and Scotland. But if only girls were born, then the girls would succeed to the throne of Scotland. There were the usual dowries to be considered, for future daughters, and for Mary if she became a widow. This was the small print of the grand marriage.

But although the delegates signed the documents, and swore fidelity to the Dauphin, the future husband of their Queen, they flatly and emphatically refused to make him co-heir to the throne of Scotland. That, they said bluntly, would cover them with infamy. Henri did not argue the point. He had, like most Renaissance princes, a trump card in his embroidered sleeve.

Two weeks before, he had persuaded Mary Stuart to sign three documents whereby the young Queen ceded to the King of France, and to his successors, her kingdom of Scotland, and all her rights to the crown of England should she die without children. Whether Henri II had it in his power to push his ambitions to the limit by force of arms was not important. For him Mary was an opportune wedge to be driven into the heart of the enemy territory of England.

Obviously it was a piece of chicanery to agree to one set of conditions of marriage with the Scottish delegates, and to induce Mary to sign away succession rights in secret documents opposed to Scottish wishes. But the princes of the Renaissance used all the weapons at their disposal and freely-signed secret documents were a comparatively small evil in a tortuous age, if thereby a prince could pull a kingdom or two from a marriage contract. These documents were to prove Mary's undoing.

They were three pieces of parchment which contributed, after many vicissitudes, to her death. She was later to contend that she had signed under duress, or at least under the hard influence of her Guise uncles. She was only a girl, she pointed out. What more natural than that she should take the advice of her close relations? At fifteen, what could she know of the implications of complicated treaties, or the sinister purport of documents she was given to sign?

Against this must be set the opinions of her uncle, the Cardinal of Lorraine. When Mary was twelve or thirteen, he wrote that she had the brain of a woman of twenty-five. This could have been a careful compliment from a doting uncle. But if she were well grounded in the arts of politics, it can be argued that she had also been well grounded in its crafts. It may have been that she was not told that she was signing away her succession rights. On the other hand, she had been schooled in the princely virtues, in grandeur, in pride of race, and in ambition. Were these three documents not the instruments of her family's pride and their ambition?

Her later protestations of youth and innocence at the time of the signature must be contrasted with the fact that, on her marriage to François, she used not only the arms of France and Scotland, but also of England and Ireland. They were engraved on her silver and tableware.

Even French historians do not entirely exonerate Mary for her part in these deceptions. Although she was in essence a French princess, she was also Queen of Scotland, and on that score she should have protected her first inheritance. In signing these three documents Mary had lent her name to duplicity, and to the cause of conflict. It was the first of her blunders.

But to Mary, in the springtime of her beauty, adored and adulated as she was at the French Court, Scotland must have seemed a far-away kingdom. It was not the most important legacy in her young mind at that moment. Scotland was hers by right of birth, France by marriage, and England could make a triple crown.

The preparation for the great marriage went forward, and when all the documents, both public and secret, had been signed the marriage was proceeded with. There was a certain precipitancy on the part of the Guise family. The bridegroom was fourteen, and already he showed signs of the tainted blood he had inherited. If the marriage could be consummated, and an heir born before this pale shadow of a Dauphin was gathered to his fathers, then the Guise family would have their sure stake in the future. The Court left Fontainebleau for Paris. The engagement was celebrated on the 19 April 1558, and on the 24 April Mary was married to François in the Cathedral of Notre Dame.

Catherine de Médicis, perhaps recalling the spectacles of Italy, the land of her birth, allied herself with the artists of the Court to make it a grandiose occasion. Outside the church a special gallery for the courtiers was erected, with a pavilion, embroidered with fleurs de lis, for the young couple. Underfoot was laid a blue carpet also embroidered with the lilies of France. At the head of the procession went musicians in doublets of scarlet and yellow, and behind them the royal cortège resplendent in silver and gold. The gallery and the pavilion were designed to give the crowd a better view of the bridal pair, and their train of courtiers. It was a spectacle not to be missed, the first royal wedding which had taken place in Paris for many years.

At the ceremony itself, all the great princes of the Church took part. In an age when church appointments were the prerogatives of the leading families, when royal bastards were rewarded with bishoprics, the pomp and riches of the Church were not neglected as sources of power. There were no complications of piety connected with the princes of the Church. At the wedding there were seventeen bishops and abbots, wearing their jewelled mitres; the Cardinal of Bourbon, assisted by the Cardinal of Lorraine, added their scarlet robes to the spectacle, and incidentally pronounced the nuptial blessing.

Mary, as heiress to a double throne, wore equally sumptuous robes. These are variously described as being of dove grey or blue velvet, sewn with pearls, and lined with white satin. Some chroniclers choose to see her as dressed in white, like the lily of France to which the poets compared her. Her train was twelve yards long. In the dark sombreness of Notre Dame, lit only by candles and reflected light through stained-glass windows, she must have seemed a symbol of youth, and of hope.

Brantôme says lyrically: 'She appeared, a hundred times more beautiful than a heavenly divinity.' She was nearly fifteen and a half.

And now, married to the Dauphin of France, she came out into the April day, while the herald at arms threw handfuls of silver and gold pieces amongst the waiting multitudes, shouting, 'Largesse, largesse,

largesse!' at which the plaudits of the crowd rang loudly, since crowds which are deluged with largesse are inclined to wish royal couples well.

The Venetian Ambassador was impressed. He wrote:

> These nuptials were considered the most regal and triumphant of any that have been witnessed in this kingdom for many years whether from the point of view of the company, or from the pomp and riches and jewels and apparel of the lords and ladies, or from the grandeur of the banquet and the stately service of the tables, or from the costliness of the masquerades and other revels.

With a background of silk embroidered with fleurs de lis, of banquets, of gold and silver plate, quartered with the arms of France, Scotland, England, and Ireland, the feasting, the masques, and the celebrations lasted several days. Mary was Queen by right, by marriage and by inheritance. It seemed she had only to stretch out her hand and all the riches and power of her world would fall into it.

It was to be the apogee of her life. By the time the trees were bare of leaves in the same year, Queen Elizabeth held her first Privy Council.

A new planet was in the ascendant.

Chapter III

6. *Mary Stuart/François II* (Mansell Collection)

After the solemnization of the marriage, the Dauphin and his bride, as was the custom, set up a separate Court at Villers-Coterets. There does not seem to have been any doubt that Mary had a genuine affection for her young husband.

In October of that year, the Scottish envoys, having concluded their negotiations over the succession with Henri II, left for home. The return journey proved a disaster. They embarked at Dieppe, but were forced back into harbour by a tempest. On returning to port they immediately fell ill. The Bishop of Orkney, the Earl of Rothes, and Lord Fleming, as well as other members of their suite, died. The five survivors of this tragedy arrived back in Scotland, but already it was bruited abroad that the others had been poisoned by the French. In an age of scant medical knowledge attacks of food poisoning, or even typhoid, were often attributed to poison. John Knox stated categorically that the poisoning was a fact. 'For whitter it was by an italian posset, or by french fogges, or by the potage of thare potingar [he was a Frenchman] thare departit fra this lyef.' But in spite of the melancholy end of more than half the envoys, the

17

Scottish Parliament declared François and Mary joint sovereigns of Scotland.

Mary Stuart's marriage had been solemnized in the April of 1558, and later that year her dark destiny cast the first shadow. Catholic Mary Tudor died on the 17 November, while she was still negotiating peace between England, France, and Spain. The balance was tipping. Catholicism was losing its power. Naturally, the question of the English succession loomed large in the minds of the French, and especially of the Guise family. In their view, Mary Stuart was the rightful heir to the English throne because she was the grand-daughter of Margaret Tudor, while Elizabeth had been declared illegitimate by her own father.

There were two courses open to the French King, and to Mary. To acknowledge freely that Elizabeth was Queen of England by right, and in fact, or to deny her rights to the throne, and invade England from France and from Scotland.

Then another fatal mistake was made. Mary and her French advisers took no firm decision—but on the advice of the King, Mary added the arms of England and Scotland to her escutcheon itself, and later to official documents signed by her she added the empty words 'Queen of France, Scotland, England and Ireland'. Mary had made her claim to the English throne, but it was a claim founded on paper, and painted on wood. Although Henri II continued to write to Elizabeth as to a fellow sovereign, his daughter-in-law continued to use the arms of England. It was a blunder which Elizabeth never forgave. In an age when kings were regarded as semi-divine, the anointed of God, this slur, and the taint of illegitimacy, were never to be forgotten by the English Queen.

Mary and the Dauphin were loaded with empty honours, but the real power still lay in the hands of the King's mistress, Diane de Poitiers, Duchesse de Valentinois. She was a clever woman of undoubted talents, and had directed the course of the King's influence for nearly twenty years, during which time the humiliation of the Queen, Catherine de Médicis, had been complete. But in July 1559, as a result of a blow from a lance in a joust, the King was mortally wounded. It was not only the end of the reign of Henri II, but also of Diane de Poitiers. The ambitions of the Guise family had come to fruition, their niece was now Queen, the lever by which they would control France. And although henceforth the faulty signature at the bottom of parchments was that of King François II, the reality was the power of Mary's uncles. François II was anointed King in Rheims by the Cardinal of Lorraine on the 18 September. The Guise triumph was complete.

François was sickly from the moment he ascended the throne. To reinforce their power over him, the Guise uncles were quick to turn him against his Bourbon relations, telling him to keep the Prince of Condé and the King of Navarre away from the Court 'because, seeing that he, François was of a delicate constitution and childless, with brothers still infants, they might be tempted to abridge their road to the throne'.

Insinuations of poison and ambushes were not the kind of intelligence calculated to improve the well-being of the frail consort of Mary Stuart, or indeed add to her own peace of mind. Mary was fond of her sickly husband, but it was also in her own interest and for the furtherance of her ambitions that he should live. His life was the guarantee of her splendour and her future.

By the end of 1559, a conspiracy against the Guise family was taking shape. The Prince of Condé was determined to use the grievances of the Huguenots to his own advantage. By January 1560, the rumours of the conspiracy were so widespread that the Guise family had to act. The royal family were at Blois with the young queen, who is described as pale, ill-looking, and extremely thin, but gracious and charming. In spite of the advice of his doctors that he should stay at Blois for his health, François was rushing frenetically from place to place hunting, first to Marchenoir, then to Châteaudun, then back to Blois, where he 'became bored with the spectacle of his court surrounded by suppliants' and went to Amboise.

François was more interested in killing deer and wild boar than in rumours of conspiracies, or even the indisposition of Mary Stuart, who was following the journeyings of her husband with difficulty. When the King, the Queens, and the Guise family with their cortège entered Amboise on the 22 February, the young Queen was described as '*souffrante*'. During her life, from puberty onwards, Mary is often described as being ill. Recent researches have suggested that Mary might have suffered from porphyria, an illness which manifests itself in gastric and hysterical symptoms. It is hard at this distance of time to judge whether her symptoms

7. *Amboise* (Mansell Collection)

were originally brought on or accentuated by the alarm and fear which surrounded her at this point in her life, for already the depth of the conspiracy had been made clear by the taking and torturing of suspects.

The Guise family were prey to conflicting counsels, some feeling that outright clemency could win the rebels over, others suggesting bargaining with them. Fantastic rumours were circulating amongst the rebels themselves, that huge numbers of Protestants were preparing to attack the Guise family, that the children of Henri II had leprosy, that the Queen Mother was the concubine of the Cardinal of Lorraine, and that he also had incestuous relations with his niece, Mary Stuart, in order to beget an heir to the throne. The populace of the Renaissance was not delicate in its accusations against its rulers.

By the middle of the month, certain prisoners were taken who pronounced with religious fervour that their aim was the total extermination of the royal family, and although others said there was no question of assassinating the King, his brothers, Queen Catherine, or Queen Mary Stuart, terror gained ground at the Court. Everyone spoke of escaping.

François II addressed an appeal to his officers and bishops, giving an amnesty to those who gave themselves up. As late as the 16 March, even the English ambassador admitted that there had been neither a sentence of death nor an execution. But at dawn the following day, while the Court was sleeping, two hundred mounted men began to attack the Château. On the 17 March the Duc de Guise was given full powers as Lieutenant General of the Kingdom, and the counter-attack began. The rebels, their plans hopelessly betrayed, started to disperse. They were hunted down remorselessly, over the countryside, and now the Guise family reacted with true ferocity against the rebels, and the executions began. They hanged the leaders of the artisans, leaders to whom only a few days before François had given alms. They hanged other prisoners without trial, and attached the corpses to the crenellations of the terrace dominating the little street of the town. Owing to the shortage of gibbets, numbers of the rebels were tied up in sacks and thrown into the Loire which was awash with corpses. The nobles and gentlemen who were in the conspiracy were beheaded in the courtyard of the Château. A contemporary writer says: 'Those of Guise reserved the leaders until after dinner, in order to afford some pastime to the ladies, and they and the ladies placed themselves at the windows, as though it had been a question of enjoying the sight of some mummery.'

Catherine, the Queen Mother, was full of the spirit of revenge, which was not altogether surprising since pamphlets calling her a whore had been found in her room. She encouraged her son to punish the rebels without pity, and from then on the executions were redoubled. Not a solitary voice was raised for the victims, not even, as far as is known, the voice of Mary Stuart. Yet according to one historian Mary Stuart certainly had nothing to do with this appalling slaughter, and it was not sure that she saw the brutalities. Brantôme says that she had a horror of blood: 'Never was this Queen cruel. She never took part in any cruelty in France, and she never took pleasure in or had the heart to watch the punishment of criminals or see them being brought to justice as some great ladies I have known.' Other historians state categorically that Mary Stuart watched the executions with queenly sang-froid.

Wherever the truth lies, misted by time, often distorted by partisanship, there can be little doubt that the terrible events at Amboise were a naked manifestation of the realities of monarchical power. When the sovereign speaks, men must obey, and if need be, men must die. In the last resort, the will of the anointed prince is supreme, must be supreme, and must be seen to be supreme. Such was the lesson Mary Stuart learnt at Amboise in the bloody spring of 1560.

The sixteenth century was an age of grandeur and cruelty, and the Guise family had acted in its spirit when they had put down the rebellion with a merciless hand. Yet Mary Stuart was also 'of the blood', her mother was sister to the men who had acted with such ferocity. Possibly there were in her the same streaks of alternating indecision and feverish activity, of feelings of forgiveness and bloodthirsty revenge.

The young Queen had now seen avuncular ambition, arrogance, and ruthlessness at work. Worse, she had seen it succeed.

Chapter IV

8. *Mary of Lorraine* (Scottish National Portrait Gallery)

By the end of 1560, the future of the Queen began to look less dazzling. In the summer of that year her mother died, worn out with the religious wars, and the factions and treacheries of the Scots. The Protestant Lords of the Congregation had deposed her as Queen Regent, and then, with some presumption, acting in the name of François and Mary, signed the Treaty of Edinburgh with England, by which they agreed to cease using the arms of England, and called a Parliament with full power to solve the religious question, and allow the reformed religion to flourish in Scotland. Whereupon the Catholic lords prudently changed sides, and finally abandoned the Queen Regent.

The Queen Regent died and, after her death, Nicholas Throckmorton, Elizabeth's Ambassador to France, tried to persuade Mary to ratify the Treaty of Edinburgh. Mary was quite clear in her ideas about her status and that of her subjects. She said calmly:

> The answer which the King, my husband, and his counsellors have given you ought to suffice, but so that you shall know that I am right to act as I do, I will make clear my reasons for refusing. My subjects in Scotland in no part do

their duty, they have kept none of their pledges. I am their Queen, they call me Queen, but they act as if I were not, they only do what they please. Those few amongst them who have remained true to me were not at their Assembly when they made all these changes. I will convene them in virtue of my authority; then they can proceed according to the laws of the kingdom, of which they continually speak, but which they do not observe.

She then referred with scorn to Sir James Sandilands as 'a poor gentleman' whom the Scots had sent her as an envoy, while to Queen Elizabeth they had sent much grander representatives. 'Is it in this way they honour me, their Queen? They must learn their duty,' she said scornfully. There spoke the voice of the dominant Guise. Indeed, when Throckmorton tried to flatter her, she remained adamant, saying, 'My uncles have spoken to you on these matters, and that should suffice.'

If she had clear ideas of her status as Queen, she had scant knowledge of the realities of power in her distant grey kingdom, nor had she any knowledge of the warring factions and blood feuds which were its components. Backed by the power of her uncles and the riches of France, the issue seemed to her clear and simple. Scotland was a remote part of her dowry.

Her Guise uncles, for their part, were now much engaged in putting down the Protestant conspiracy. On the 30 August, after the events at Amboise, they decided to take advantage of François' anger against the malcontents. The Estates were to be summoned to Orléans, the heart of the Protestant religion, and an exemplary punishment was to be meted out to the rebel city.

After certain elementary precautions, such as disarming the citizenry, it was announced that François and Mary were preparing to make their official entrance into the town on the 17 October. The town officials were given to understand that the young King and Queen expected a reception which by its splendour and by the amount of assiduity shown would touch the heart of the King, and soften his anger against the rebellious town. At the same time as orders for grandeur, various inspired sources were circulating other less amusing snippets of information. It was said 'that it was necessary to push justice to its fullest limits, and that the King was furiously angered against the town, that he held its inhabitants for mortal enemies, and had pondered putting to death its principal citizens'. The rumour added, with clear French logic, that their goods 'were already bespoken to various courtiers'.

While the town of Orléans nervously planned a gala reception, the King and Queen were proceeding from St Germain-en-Laye through Paris with an escort of footguards, cavalry, knights, and twelve hundred men of the gendarmerie who had sworn themselves to the service of the Duc de Guise.

Word was sent to the royal party that the citizens were beginning to respond to this policy of suggestions and threats. On the 18 October, with drums and fifes, and flags flying, the different groups of townspeople formed up and awaited the royal party. They halted under a carpeted gallery ornamented with crests and escutcheons. Under orders, the town had done the King and Queen proud. Opening the march was a force large enough to be colourful but small enough to be unprovocative— 440 arquebusiers of the town, dressed in black, and 350 seamen armed with pikes and halberds, marching five by five. Then came the trade of the town, barrelmakers, winemakers, masons, carpenters, pastry cooks, jewellers, shoemakers, everyone down to the simpler trades of butchers, bakers, and candlestick-makers. The corporations were said to be so numerous that if the banners had been carried one by one it would have taken five hours for them to pass, so they marched in threes. Behind the trade came the town archers, the clerks dressed in velvet and satin of grey and gold, the notaries, the lawyers, the Chief Magistrate, the officials of the University, the rector and eight doctors in scarlet robes, some enriched with precious stones. The magistrates, clothed in black velvet, mounted on fine horses, formed a small separate procession, giving the King the keys of the town and expressing their good wishes and fealty to him.

François II, mounted on his horse, then made his official entry into Orléans under a canopy of cloth of gold embroidered with the arms of the town, carried by four of the magistrates. Around him were grouped the Dukes of Orléans and Angoulême, the Prince de la Roche sur Yon, several great lords of the Orders of Knights, two hundred gentlemen of the Household, the Swiss, and the arquebusiers. All the approaches were decorated with triumphal arches, and anxious cries of 'Long Live the King' rang out, while in the distance the town guns boomed out their welcome, and possibly also their warning that retribution might be at hand if loyalty should prove frail.

The King proceeded to the Cathedral, where he heard an address of welcome from the Bishop, and the procession re-formed to conduct the King to his lodgings in the centre of the town.

After the official dinner, the same procedure, the same parade of honours took place for the official reception of the Queen, Mary Stuart. She entered the town surrounded by princesses and duchesses of the Court, riding on snow-white palfreys. A contemporary writes that she was 'so admirably beautiful that, if the silver moon herself had appeared glittering, surrounded by its attendant stars, the moon would have appeared tarnished beside such rare perfection and shining beauty'.

The only non-participants at these grand official entries were its 'onlie begetters', the Duc de Guise and the Cardinal of Lorraine. Some said that, modestly, they did not want to draw attention to themselves on the great day, others, less friendly, alleged that they feared assassination.

The splendour of the welcome from the Orléannais at first seemed somewhat to have softened the anger of the King against the Protestant town. But behind the cordial face of the King, the Guises, whose constant obsession was the suppression of heresy, had manned the squares and gates of the town with picked men; as well as four companies of veteran soldiers, there were four thousand Germans ready to proceed against the local citizenry. Further measures were the ominous preparations of auxiliary prisons, and the precautionary interception of all correspondence.

Nevertheless, the two Bourbons, the King of Navarre and the Prince of Condé, decided to grasp the nettle. They arrived at Orléans on the 30 October. The interview with François II reads like a scene from Shakespeare. The two uncles, waiting in the embrasure of a window, 'watched and encouraged the King with their looks'. The Court waited while the King of Navarre went into the hall, bowing many times, even putting his knee to the ground. François remained impassive. Apparently it was only with the greatest difficulty that he managed to lift the hat he was wearing. When in his turn Condé came in the King did not take off his hat, and Condé was arrested and thrown into prison.

It could be said that the political education of Mary Stuart took place in a hard and curious school. The politics of the Renaissance, as practised by the Guise family, were a compound of intimidation, cruelty, the use of grandeur to cover the naked show of force, the embroidered velvet glove hiding a hand which did not shrink from bloodshed. Whether the blood was innocent or guilty was not important to a generation which upheld its politics and its religions literally to the death. To whom death would come was a question which was always in the balance. Now the Guise family held the triumphant sword. One of their first acts on arriving at Orléans was to institute a tribunal of the Holy Office charged with prosecuting those suspected of the crime of heresy. The Cardinal and the Duc had a free hand because the King had gone off hunting, as usual, leaving his uncles to conduct 'serious business'.

The Protestant historians allege that thirty or forty executioners were assembled, who paraded round the town dressed in livery, and that the scaffold destined for Condé was set up in front of the King's lodging. Citizens were forbidden to leave their houses once midday had struck, or even to look out of their windows. A contemporary gives details of a vast massacre of the Reformed Church which was planned not only at Orléans but all through France, 'thanks to incitement from priests and monks the great greyhound would be unleashed upon the flesh of the Protestants, and would achieve their extermination'.

If Mary had the brain of a woman of twenty-five at the age of fifteen, at the age of eighteen she cannot have been ignorant of the atmosphere of the town which had welcomed her with such pomp. Fear is communicable. She had seen the rebellion at Amboise put down without mercy. Now she saw what intimidation and guile seemed about to accomplish.

But the Guise triumph was short-lived. On the 17 November, the feast of St Aignan, coming out of Vespers, François felt a sudden pain in his head. It was quickly realized that the King's illness was serious. On the 2 December, a solemn procession was held to implore heaven for a cure.

On the 3 December, the Guises spoke of the King with tears in their eyes, as well they might.

But in spite of the prayers, the vows, and the hopes of the Guise family, François II died on the 5 December. In the words of Throckmorton, he 'went to God', and with him went the hopes, the splendours, and the future of Mary Stuart.

'God deprived me of everything which I loved and held dear in this world,' Mary wrote, 'leaving me the consolation, such as it is, that I see those around who weep for his lot, and my great sadness.'

Locally, those who wept were not numerous. The satisfaction of the Protestants was heartfelt. Calvin wrote: 'Have you ever heard anything more opportune than the death of the little King? God struck the father in the eye, and the son in the ear.' The Orléannais of the Reformed Church sang a solemn canticle for 'the deliverance which God has given his people on the 5 December 1560. From time to time, and year to year, sing to God of his great and unique bounty that on this day he has spared the City from a furious enemy planning to make it a prey to every wickedness and cruelty.'

A palace revolution followed the last sigh of François II, and it was not a revolution in favour of Mary, the dethroned widow.

Chapter V

9. *Catherine de Médicis* *(Courtauld Institute of Art)*

The death of François II at last gave Catherine de Médicis the power she had always craved. At first it was her husband's mistress, Diane de Poitiers, who in effect had reigned in her stead, then it was Mary Stuart, the stalking horse of the Guise family, wife of her eldest son. But her second son, Charles IX, was a minor, so it was her turn to taste true power.

From the moment of the death of François II, it was clear that everything had changed. The fortunes of the Guise family were falling, and with them the fortunes of Mary Stuart. Catherine was quick to seize not only power but the symbols of power. She demanded the great seals from the Cardinal of Lorraine. And just as she had acted with Diane de Poitiers, so she acted with Mary Stuart, the King's widow, demanding back the Crown Jewels on the day of the King's death. There were no niceties observed, the threat was already apparent.

Mary obviously realized that her days at the French Court were numbered. Her mother-in-law was her enemy and had not forgotten a remark by her daughter-in-law that Catherine was descended from shopkeepers. Mary detached herself from the Court, 'but little by little, so that it did not seem that she had been forcibly pushed out'. The young widow went to pass the remainder of the winter with her aunt, Renée de Lorraine, who was abbess of a convent at Rheims. There she had plenty of time to reflect on her situation. As far as remaining in France was concerned, the outlook was bleak.

When the Earl of Bedford, Elizabeth's envoy, arrived to offer Mary condolences on the death of her husband, he also brought advice from England, and a renewed demand to ratify the Treaty of Edinburgh. The meeting between Mary Stuart, Throckmorton, the Ambassador, and Bedford, the special envoy, must have been a classic example of defence in depth on her part. It is impossible not to admire the courteous and consummate skill with which the girl took refuge behind her uncles in order to gain time. The English envoy having made clear what his instructions were, Mary replied that 'she took in good part the counsels of her sister, the Queen of England, that she would follow them in everything, being persuaded that they would be to her profit'. She went on to speak of her situation, of the need which she had of good advice and friendship, of her desire of allying herself with Elizabeth, and of the reasons which ought to ally them to one another in an *entente cordiale*. She went on to assure the English envoy of her sincere feelings towards Elizabeth. 'I will fulfil towards the Queen of England, and I wish that she will be so assured, all the good offices of a sincere friend, good sister, and neighbour, and I expect that she will act in the same way towards me.'

Good sense dictated this policy to Mary Stuart, but it was a policy which she was never to implement. Instead she prevaricated. She drew attention to her weakness and her dependence on other people.

> I am here, as you see, without counsel. My uncle, the Cardinal, who directs all my affairs, and whom it is my duty to consult, is absent at this moment. Also, monsieur l'ambassadeur, the advice of your mistress, my good sister, is that I should take counsel of the nobles and wise men of my kingdom, as you told me not long since. As you know, I have none near me, but I await them. Then I can make a reply to your mistress which will satisfy her.

Bedford insisted that she was held on her honour, and that in fact she owed the Queen of England this proof of her sincerity. Mary again fell back on her charm and her womanly weakness. 'Alas, my lord,' she replied, 'what can I do, alone as I am? The ratification of a treaty is a great affair, especially for a princess of my age.'

'But, Madame,' replied Throckmorton, 'you have here M. de Guise, your other uncle, whose advice up to now you have been happy to take, new delays are not possible, with so many promises which have been given so often that the treaty would be ratified.'

Again Mary cleverly fell back behind the shadow of others. 'What was done in the lifetime of my husband,' she replied, 'you cannot put to my charge, I was then under his orders. Today I would be loath to act lightly, and as this is a grave matter, I ask you for some delay until I have taken Counsel.'

Having drawn a blank the two English representatives retired, but the Queen recalled Throckmorton and reproached him playfully that he had

Mary of Guise, attributed to Corneille de Lyon (Scottish National Portrait Gallery)

Mary, Queen of Scots, by unknown artist in Huntly House, Edinburgh (City Museums, Edinburgh)

COR VNVM V A VN

not brought her a portrait of his mistress, Queen Elizabeth. 'I attach great importance to this, and I ask you, monsieur l'ambassadeur, to get it for me, I am more than ever desirous of having it, and the time seems long to me until I shall have received it.'

She could be playful and cozening over the small things, but sent the ambassador away empty-handed over the large matter of the Treaty. For a young woman engaged in one of her first diplomatic skirmishes her conduct was nothing less than brilliant.

At Vitry, Mary received Lord James Stuart, her bastard brother, who had been sent to her as envoy from Scotland. For Mary it was an ill-starred meeting. As a prelude to his visit, he had had the prudence to call on Queen Elizabeth and William Cecil. English historians depict Cecil as a clever, patient, astute politician, the trusty and trusted right hand of his Queen. The French, on the other hand, paint him as '*brutalement anglais*', a fox of whom Mary was the victim.

At her meeting with her brother, Mary confided to him that she would never give her approval of the Treaty of Edinburgh, which had been concluded without a mandate from her and in contempt of all her rights. Unfortunately for Mary, James Stuart hurried to make a new stay in London before returning to his native Scotland. Doubtless he revealed all. He was a man who preferred to keep in with both sides, and in a politically unstable age it was the way to survive.

But in spite of her negotiations for her return to Scotland, it was apparent that her sadness and her repugnance at the prospect grew deeper. Brantôme, then a young page attached to the house of Guise, prophetically writes, 'How many times I have seen her apprehensive, as if of death, of this journey. Desiring a hundred times more to stay in France as a simple dowager than to go and reign in her wild country.'

As her departure grew closer she asked Elizabeth's permission to pass through England. The reply was uncompromising. Ratify the Treaty of Edinburgh, and Mary would receive all the facilities and honours due to her. If not, the safe conduct would not be forthcoming. In her last interview with Throckmorton before leaving, she said:

> I hope that the wind will be favourable and that I shall not have to land on the coast of England; if I do land, monsieur l'ambassadeur, your queen will have me in her hands, and will be able to do with me what she wills. If she is so cruel as to wish my death, let her have her pleasure, let her sacrifice me. Perhaps this destiny will serve me better than life. The will of God be done.

What mood was this? The petulance or arrogance of a Guise, a flash of hot temper from her Scottish blood, or a mixture of both followed by an uncanny glimpse of a dreadful day still so many troubled years ahead?

Mary then stayed for some time at St Germain-en-Laye to make her adieux to the royal family. She delayed at Abbeville, unwilling to embark, and then finally on the 10 August, with a glittering escort of nobles and gentlemen, she arrived at Calais where the ship awaited her.

Brantôme described the departure.

The galley being gone from the port a fresh little breeze sprang up and the sails filled. The Queen had her two arms on the poop of the galley on the side of the helm, and dissolving into heavy tears, turning her beautiful eyes on the port, and the place from which she had departed, she pronounced again and again these sad heavy words: 'Adieu France!' until night fell. She had no desire to eat, and would not go down into the poop cabin, so they made her a bed on deck. She commanded the helmsman that as soon as it was day, and he saw the coast of France again, that he would awaken her, and not fail to call her. In this fortune was in her favour because the wind dropped, and the sailors had to have recourse to the oars, and little progress was made that night. The day appearing, the coast of France still lay near the ship, and the helmsman not having failed her orders, she lifted herself on her bed, and lying there contemplated the coastline of France as long as she could, redoubling her sighs, and saying these words over and over again, 'Adieu France, adieu France! I do not think I shall set eyes on your dear land again'.

Ronsard says, 'The day your sails filled with the winds you were borne away from our weeping eyes. Nothing remains but the sadness which stirs within my deepest heart for the remembrance of a princess without parallel.'

The unparalleled princess was approaching a very different country from the one which she had left. Neither her Guise blood, nor the uncritical adulation of her upbringing in France, nor the splendours of the French Court, had fitted her for it. But her physical bravery was something which nobody could take away.

She was to need it all.

Chapter VI

12. *The house of John Knox, Edinburgh* (Mansell Collection)

Mary arrived at Leith on a foggy morning of September. Her arrival was premature, and she was obliged to stay the night at Leith while her loyal subjects hurriedly made their simple preparations for her reception. Even mounts were lacking for her party. These arrived in the evening, rough hacks of the country, and when the Queen saw them she wept, humiliated that her French entourage should be aware of the poverty of her kingdom.

It was indeed very poor, as is apparent in an account of the battle of Pinkie Cleugh, which had taken place only fourteen years before. A participant at the battle complains that the lairds were as ill-dressed as the peasants, 'all clad alike in jacks covered with white leather, doublets of the same, or of fustian, no one with either chain, brooch, ring, or garment of silk that I could see'. So ill-clad were the Scottish noblemen that when the prisoners came to be counted the victors found they had taken twenty peasants to one gentleman, a cardinal error in an age of ransoms.

There is no reason to suppose that Scotland had become richer in the interim. The country to which Mary Stuart returned was a poor land riven by faction: religious faction, faction of lords against the Crown, faction of lords against other lords. The nobles, while fighting each other or the Crown, were also not averse to selling their services either to England or to France according to how fortune seemed to be running. Even the religious conflicts had a background of self-interest. Many of the revenues of the abbeys and priories had fallen into the pockets of the Scottish nobility. The Reformers had included in their reforms the sack of religious houses, and so mingled with their religious fervour a keen eye to the main chance. If they had an unwillingness to see the return of Catholicism it was certainly allied to a reluctance to give up the monetary gains which had resulted from the desecration of churches and altars.

This was the background of the Scottish Queen's inheritance. In France she had seen her uncles locked in combat with the Protestants, putting them down with force of arms. Here in Reformist Scotland she was in a strange land, without reliable allies or the support of her powerful relations. For the first time she was on her own, in deep turbulent waters.

The voice of the Reformers, John Knox, was not on her side. He was understandably no friend to the French, since his spell as a prisoner in French galleys, and like Calvin he was inclined to view the death of his enemies with satisfaction, and had hymned the death of Marie de Guise as Calvin had done the death of François II.

Jehovah was on the side of the Saints, as the Reformers called themselves. Many writers hold that John Knox found it impossible to distinguish Jehovah's voice from his own. Even the fog which shrouded the arrival of Mary's ships gave him cause for satisfaction.

> In the memory of man, that day of the year was never seen a more dolourous face of the heaven than was at her arrival. For beside the surface wet, and corruption of the air, the mist was so thick and dark, the sun was not seen to shine two days before, nor two days after. That forewarning God gave unto us, but alas, the most part were blind.

Like many plain-spoken characters he made a virtue of discourtesy, and in his eyes the Queen could do no right. He talked of the Court as being full of 'fiddlers and dancers, and to have been exercised in flinging upon a floor, and in the rest that follows', and in the patrimony of the Crown, 'given in inheritance to skippers, dancers and dalliers with dames'. Adding that that was the beginning of the reign of Mary, Queen of Scots, and 'these were the fruits she brought forth of France'. The Queen from the soft valley of the Loire had struck a northern rock against which her cozening and charm could not prevail.

From the moment of her arrival, Knox was constantly up in his plain wooden pulpit in St Giles denouncing foreign ways, foreign marriages, and the Church of Rome. Much as the Queen may have determined to pursue the middle course of religious tolerance, this was not on the programme of the Saints. Even to her face Knox harangued and denounced her, but she stood up to him with courage: 'I perceive that my subjects shall obey you, and shall do what they will, and not what I command, and so must I be subject to them, and not they to me.'

He replied: 'Let the Prince and subject both obey God. Kings should be foster-fathers of the Kirk and Queens its nursing mothers.' He was putting women in their place. She replied tartly: 'You are not of the Kirk

that I will nurse, I will defend the Kirk of Rome, for I think it is the Kirk of God.'

Encouraged by Knox the Lords of the Congregation persecuted and even killed priests. Mary had stated categorically, even before leaving France, that she would support liberty of worship amongst her subjects. But the very first Sunday after her arrival in Scotland, when Mass was being said in her private chapel, a number of the Saints assembled outside Holyrood in tumultuous protest. If they were claiming liberty of worship for themselves, they were unwilling to allow it to their Queen. Lord Lindsay, clad in armour and brandishing his sword, cried out that 'the idolatrous priest should die the death'. The protesters were prevented from entering, but it was only with difficulty that the sack of the chapel was prevented. Mary's French entourage were so disgusted with the spectacle that they wished to return to France immediately. The Queen herself, sad and pained, cried out: 'This is a fine beginning to the obedience of my subjects! I have no knowledge of how it will go, but I foresee that it will end badly.'

The man who held the door of the chapel and prevented the Saints from entering was Lord James Stuart, the Queen's bastard brother. James Stuart, afterwards Earl of Moray, was another of those ambiguous Renaissance characters whose actions were so labyrinthine that it is difficult to untangle good motives from shrewd political moves. French historians show him as a tool of Elizabeth, plotting and scheming the downfall of his sister even before her arrival in Scotland. His duplicity and lust for power are shown by them to be without bounds. Yet other historians view him with more sympathy, showing him to be a loyal brother to his sister, only abandoning her when her double dealing had made her a doubtful political asset to Scotland. Possibly the truth lies between these two views. While he may not have desired her return to Scotland, once she was there as legitimate Queen he was prepared to govern in her name. Mary had always been under the tutelage of men stronger than herself, and James Stuart was the nearest to her in blood and the most *rusé* in the understanding of the state of the factions and feuds in the country.

He was of that breed of men who had patience as well as courage, but

35

he was not averse to profiting financially from the mistakes of others. It has been said that Lord James and William Maitland of Lethington completely governed for the Queen and that this was the first of her mistakes, since she already knew of their intrigues. Possibly she hoped to attach them to her by her charm, and to outwit them.

To some historians, with hindsight, it may seem easy to decide who is the victim and who the victimizer, but to others the issue must always be in doubt. Charm, a facile cover for intrigue, makes an uneasy partner to intelligence, and it can defeat its own ends. Mary was no longer in a country whose background she understood, and while the murderous strains in France under the sway of the Guise family may have been no less violent than those in Scotland, they were used for different ends and in a different political context. Scotland had a habit of rebellion against its sovereigns, and in a wild country lords and lairds regarded themselves as petty kings. If they gave their allegiance to the Queen, it was as a favour, not a recognition of her Divine Right.

Although the years between 1561 and 1565 were peaceful on the surface, fantastically complicated plots were evolved.

In one such, at the beginning of 1562 the Earl of Bothwell appeared at the centre of an alleged scheme to kidnap the Queen, take her to Dumbarton Castle and compel her by force to marry the Earl of Arran, son of the Duke of Châtellerault. Some days after his meeting with his father, Arran wrote, denouncing the plot and his father, to the Queen. As part of the plot included the killing of Lord James Stuart, the latter had a natural interest in this piece of intelligence. But when interrogated by Lord James, Arran alleged that he had been controlled by witchcraft, and when questioned by whose witchcraft, he said that the witch was the mother of Lord James Stuart. This somewhat complicated the affair. Later Arran withdrew his accusations against his own father, but continued to hold that Bothwell had been concerned in the plot. The later history of Bothwell could lend substance to the story. Eventually the Duke of Châtellerault left his castle, where he had prudently shut himself up, came to Court, and begged the forgiveness of the Queen. He said his son was mad. Mary took no action against these two. Randolph, the English Ambassador in Scotland, writing to Cecil, acknowledged the magnanimity of Mary's attitude and commented that she was actuated by no animosity against either father or son, had treated them with goodness and even generosity, and had made it plain that she regarded them as her successors to the Crown. The case of Bothwell was more ambiguous. He was thrown into gaol, from where he escaped and sought refuge in England. The incident was a curious presage of his subsequent history.

At the beginning of her reign Mary and Elizabeth were in constant correspondence on 'dear Sister' terms. A meeting between the two Queens was constantly mooted and just as often put off. The Treaty of Edinburgh, and Mary's claims to the English throne, still hung over their relations like a cloud. Mary still temporized, asking for a revision of the treaty before a joint commission of Englishmen and Scots. Elizabeth replied: 'When princesses treat by open assembly of ambassadors, the world, especially the subjects of both, judge the amity not sound. You shall see we require nothing but justice, honour and reason.'

Mary replied in conciliatory vein, but added in characteristic style: 'We know how near we are descended of the blood of England, and what devices have been attempted to make us a stranger to it! We trust being so near your cousin ye would be loth we should receive so manifest an injury as utterly to be debarred from that title which in all possibility may fall unto us.'

This was not a tactful reply to a Queen who was unwilling even to hear talk of possible successors. And although Mary added, 'If we had such a matter to treat with any other prince, there is no person whose advice we should rather follow,' the 'dear Sisters' were never to meet. Elizabeth seized the excuse of the outbreak of the Civil War in France to break off negotiations. Mary suffered a cruel disappointment, and heard the excuses of the English Ambassador with tears in her eyes.

To assuage her disappointment she turned her eyes north, and decided to visit the most remote parts of her kingdom. This journey was undertaken in bitter weather. Randolph writes that it was a terrible journey which had been decided on by the Queen rather than approved by her advisers. She had never feared physical exertions. But the planned royal progress turned into a campaign.

Sir John Gordon, son of the Earl of Huntly, the most powerful of all the Catholic nobles, had been brawling over some lawsuit in the streets of Edinburgh, and nearly killed Lord Ogilvy. He was thrown into prison, and escaped to take refuge with his powerful father, head of the Gordon clan, who were now in open revolt against the Queen. She rode north against them. It has been suggested that Lord James Stuart urged her on to this campaign because he was anxious to get possession of the Huntly lands.

The Queen rode into Inverness and demanded entrance to the Castle. This was refused, but on learning that the Queen had a large force with her, the Earl of Huntly surrendered the Castle. The captain who had originally refused her entrance was hanged; a daughter of the Guise family was not given to tolerating obstruction from underlings.

She did not find campaigning arduous. One English observer remarked:

> In all these broils I assure you I never saw her merrier, never dismayed, nor never thought that so much stomach to be in her that I find. She repented nothing, but (when the lords and others at Inverness came in the morning from the watch), that she was not a man, to know what life it was to lie all night in the fields, or to walk on the causeway with a jack and a knapsack, a Glasgow buckler and a broad sword.

The Queen rode into Aberdeen, but Huntly changed his policy and again decided to raise his clans against her. At Corrichie, about twelve miles from Aberdeen, he encountered the forces of the Queen. The battle was soon over. Huntly fell dramatically from his horse, dead from a coronary or a stroke. His body was put on to a cart and cast into prison. Subsequently it was gruesomely judged, and condemned to death, being propped up in the court, while the Queen in royal robes sat in judgement on it.

His son, Sir John Gordon, was condemned to death. The Queen witnessed the execution, according to some chroniclers, under the duress of Lord James. Others see in her harsh action the use of execution as an instrument of policy. The young man, at the moment of putting his head on the block, looked up at the Queen, causing the executioner to make several false strokes. The Queen shrieked and fainted.

But was she, as Brantôme said, incapable of cruel actions? The story of the unfortunate Chastelard seems to belie this. Again the issues are confused. Chastelard had been one of the poets who had followed Mary to Scotland, subsequently returning to France with the other French lords. The reasons for his return to Scotland are given variously, some saying that he was lured by his intense passion for the Queen, others that the outbreak of the Civil War in France was the cause of his return. He was well received by the Queen, recalling to her perhaps the softer and more cultivated airs of the French Court. He accompanied her on the lute when she sang, and partnered her in the dancing so disapproved of by Knox.

According to Knox, 'Chastelard was so familiar in the Queen's cabinet that scarcely could any of the Nobility have access to her. The Queen would lie upon Chastelard's shoulder, and sometimes privily she would steal a kiss of his neck. And this was honest enough; for it was the gentle entreatment of a stranger.'

Whether the Queen's easy manners were misunderstood by the lovesick poet, or whether he took a Frenchman's practical view of the outcome of the affair, the upshot was unfortunate. He hid himself under the Queen's bed. Here he was found, according to some accounts by her ladies and according to others by her grooms of the chamber, and chased out. The Queen was told the next day, and the poet was ordered to leave Scotland in twenty-four hours. In a country dominated by the opinions of Knox, she had no wish for a scandal.

But the poet was not so easily discouraged. The following day, when she left Edinburgh, Chastelard followed her, and concealed himself in her bedroom again. When she was about to undress he rushed from his hiding place, some say to demand pardon, others to declare his undying love, and others to rape the Queen. She screamed for help, and when Lord James came to her aid she said: 'Thrust your dagger into the villain!' This remark has a curious echo of Shakespeare's Beatrice saying: 'Kill Claudio.' The affront to the person of the anointed sovereign, and to the pride of the daughter of 'ceux des Guises', demanded instant death.

Lord James, more prudent than his volatile sister, said 'it would not be

38

for her honour if he were punished by a summary act of vengeance, but that he must be dealt with according to the laws of the realm'.

According to Knox, Lord James pleaded for the life of the poet, and he insinuates that Mary was unwilling for Chastelard to be brought to public trial for fear he should reveal a scandal against the Queen. He was summarily tried and condemned to death. It was a harsh end, and Mary was adamant in her refusal to accord him any mercy. This refusal is in curious contrast to Brantôme's descriptions of her softness and tender ways. On the other hand, Randolph remarked on 'that majesty that I have seen in her, and that modesty that I have wondered to be in her'. Possibly both the majesty and the modesty had been offended, and her pride had struck back with the iron hand of her Guise blood.

Chastelard died with panache, refusing religious consolation, reciting Ronsard's *Ode to Death*, and turning towards the windows where he thought Mary was lodged, said in a loud voice: 'Adieu, the most beautiful and the most cruel Princess in the world.' Was it a romantically tragic story, or a political manœuvre? Lethington later said that Chastelard admitted that he had been sent from France by 'persons of distinguished position to sully the honour of the Queen'. The suggestion was that he was a Huguenot. It is not surprising that the sixteenth century loved a maze in their gardens—it was a symbol of their intricate minds.

Knox, as usual, found food for uplift in the death of Chastelard, stating that he 'received the reward of his dancing, for he lacked his head that his tongue should not utter the secrets of our Queen'.

Chapter VII

15. *Henri, Duc de Guise* (Mansell Collection)

The cradle of Mary Stuart was shadowed by offers of marriage. Her widowhood was even more clouded. The number of offers, and supposed offers, ranged from the King of Denmark, the King of Sweden, the son of the Count Palatine, the Archduke of Austria, and most important of all, Don Carlos, the heir to Philip II of Spain.

Mary's dilemma was that of a woman crossing a frail bridge from one shore to another. If she looked backward to the Continent she had left, the glittering prize of the Catholic throne of Spain glimmered faintly; but before her, glowing equally dimly, lay the throne of England to which she considered herself the rightful heir. In the centre, Scotland itself was divided between Catholics and Protestants.

Now from France tragic news arrived. Her uncle, the Duc de Guise, was assassinated; another uncle, the Duc d'Aumale, had died in battle. The guiding lights of her youth were being extinguished one by one.

She eventually turned her eyes again to Spain, where Philip II agreed in principle that the marriage would be a good thing 'in the interest of religion', a sentiment hardly flattering to Mary, the fairest flower of France. But Cecil's spies got wind of the affair, and Randolph was sent to express Elizabeth's intense displeasure at the idea of a foreign marriage.

Knox also entered the lists. He was, as usual, inspired by the Almighty to draw the attention of the nobles and the Queen to the path of duty, and the path of duty was, of course, to be mapped out by Knox. Now he thundered that if one of the ungodly, and all papists were ungodly, should become the master of the Queen, then all the nobles would have contributed to banish Christ from the realm, and to bring down the vengeance of God on the country and on themselves.

Mary sent for Knox and in a furious passion said with some reason that no prince had ever been treated as she had been: 'I have borne with you in all your rigorous manner of speaking both against myself and against my uncles, yea, I have sought your favour by all possible means: I offered unto you presence and audience, whensoever it pleased you to admonish me, and yet I cannot be quit of you. I vow to God I shall be once revenged.'

Knox said that once he was up in the pulpit he was no longer master of his speech but had to obey God, who commanded him to preach the truth. It was a good alibi, and unanswerable. He went on to say that a foreign marriage would endanger the independence of the country, and bring no profit to the Queen. She dissolved into tears and told him to leave. He was not daunted and on leaving contented himself with remarking to the Court ladies that their fresh and tender flesh would shortly be devoured by worms. He himself presumably was not averse to fresh and tender flesh, since he married a girl of sixteen when he was fifty-eight.

Whether because of the difficulties pressing upon her, or the deaths of her uncles, Mary sank into a depression. Randolph, the English Ambassador, found her ill, and wrote that for two months the Queen had fallen into melancholy, her grief seemed to be secret, and she often cried without apparent reason. Her illness became worse every day and she complained of a pain in her right side: even when she was well she took no pleasure in company. Were these the symptoms of porphyria as some have suggested, or was it a form of nervous reaction brought on by her difficulties with her rebellious subjects? Mary had started with much in her favour, and now she found herself in a hostile country, a cold climate, with little comfort, and only advisers whom she suspected.

It was unfortunate for Randolph that Mary should have been indisposed. His mission was delicate, none other than to propose to the Queen, a husband—the favourite of Elizabeth, Robert Dudley, Earl of Leicester. Mary had once described Dudley as Elizabeth's horsemaster, and she was not likely to be overjoyed at this suggestion. The bait to be held out was that Elizabeth would immediately agree to Mary's claim to succeed to the English throne should she marry Dudley. At first the name of the candidate for Mary's hand was kept secret, and she imagined that it must be Lord Darnley, who had both English and Scottish blood, and a distant claim to the English throne. Failing a more brilliant union, Darnley could have advantages, and he was not a foreigner, which could please the Scots, even conceivably John Knox. If Elizabeth now wished to take a hand in Mary's marriage project, and had decided to promote her own candidate, her favourite, Leicester, what was the reason? The

humiliation of Mary, or some devious idea that in this way she could make Dudley a king without marrying him, and bind Scotland to England by sentiment alone? The puzzle has never been resolved.

Mary listened with patience to Randolph's proposals. After certain sharp exchanges, she said that she took Elizabeth's offer rather as witnessing her goodwill than a proof of her sincerity because, she implied, Elizabeth would never be able to separate herself from Dudley. But Mary, still with her eyes on the English throne, did not give a definite answer. When she sought to do so it was too late.

The Spanish marriage had been finally rejected by Philip II, and Mary turned her eyes speculatively to Darnley. De Silva, the Spanish Ambassador in London, wrote in the September of 1564 that he had been sent instructions 'to keep a sharp look-out on the affairs of Scotland, as although the two Queens correspond, and keep each other in play until one or the other of them shows her hand, they both go in fear, and will give but short grace'. The picture presented is of two careful, sleek cats, and the mice were their marriage suitors, of whom Darnley was now one.

Robert Dudley, Earl of Leicester, had slipped through the matrimonial net. Unknown to Randolph, somewhere along the line something had gone wrong. Either Elizabeth had changed her mind for feminine reasons, or Leicester had changed his mind for reasons of fear or greater ambition. Marriage with Mary could bring eventual perils.

At this juncture Darnley was allowed by Elizabeth to go to Scotland.

Some historians allege that Elizabeth permitted this journey in the fore-knowledge that he was of a weak and vicious character, and consequently would be a disruptive element in the affairs of Scotland. In 1564 Randolph wrote: 'I am evil willing that my Lord of Darnley should come hither' because he feared that Elizabeth would be blamed for sending 'so great a plague into this country'. At least Randolph had no illusions about Darnley's character.

But in spite of her thoughts turning toward Darnley, Mary had not entirely given up Leicester as a means of furthering her ambitions. Unaware, apparently, that Elizabeth or Leicester, or both, had changed their minds, she had indeed given Randolph to understand that at long last she was in favour of the Leicester match, and the unfortunate Ambassador, who earlier had come out firmly in favour of it, now had to back-pedal as best he could. He was forced to write letters of apology. To Cecil he wrote: 'I so much overshot myself and your Honour in my last letters that I repent they escaped my hand.' In this letter to Leicester a sudden gleam of weary truth appears. 'I would that I might, with much more earnest travail than ever your Lordship took in this matter, marry but some good old widow that had wherewith to keep me towards my old days.'

Randolph now had the unpleasant task of telling the Queen of Scots that the wind had changed. He writes to Leicester: 'I could not so cunningly handle the matter, nor temper it with such terms, but I might perceive in her, in my tale-telling, that altogether she grew discontented.' This was an understatement. Mary was furiously angry and ended her tirade: 'I will not fail in any good offices towards my sister, your mistress, but trust much from henceforth for that matter I will not.'

The Ambassador adds: 'I sought to mitigate that choler but nothing would serve at that time. She had taken her horse and rideth a hunting. I tarried to talk with my Lord of Moray. What shall I say but that I found him almost stark mad?'

He then had further chat with Lethington and Moray. 'The Queen returned from her pastimes. I perceived more sadness in her look than countenance amiss towards me. She retires to her cabinet; and I again to my two good lords.'

He did little good there, and ended his description of the interview: 'I know not of us all three who was most angry.' He tried to patch the matter up with Moray, and even went to Moray's lodgings after the Sunday sermon. But Moray had not calmed down. 'The devil cumber you, our Queen doth nothing but weep and write. Amend this betimes or all will be nought,' he said. Again the Ambassador tried to say that 'all things should be well'.

'It passeth my power,' said Moray. The English Ambassador reported bitterly: 'So it did mine.'

Lethington was also not on the Ambassador's side, for Randolph reported that 'he cursed me that could guide a Queen no better when I had her in my will, but so handle her that she must be fain to put herself into her enemies hands'.

Both Moray and Lethington were learning the measure of the Queen's charm, caprices, and choler, and feared her precipitate actions. It is assumed by many writers that Mary, furious, turned to Darnley as a sop to her wounded pride. She had not been happy in her suitors. The Earl of Arran was mad, and Don Carlos was a maniac. The sickly François II, who had elevated her to the splendour to which her mind often returned, was in his grave.

Darnley was to prove as frail a reed as the others.

Queen Elizabeth I, by Zucchero (by permission of Mrs P. A. Tritton, Parham, Sussex, and Trans-Globe)

Chapter VIII

17. *Henry, Lord Darnley* (British Museum)

The shifts and caprices of the two Queens involving Mary's marriage to Darnley are as intricate as the characters of the women themselves. The facts are that Darnley was allowed to go to Scotland by Elizabeth, and that very shortly afterwards Mary married him. Her motives for the sudden marriage appear equally confused. Historians and romanticists are at odds over Mary's supposed infatuation for Darnley. Zweig came down on the side of awakening sexual passion: 'She wished to bestow her young body freely. She only heard the pulsing of her blood, and obeyed the desire and will of her senses.' Another writer starts with listing all the political advantages of the Darnley marriage, and says that possibly her heart had fallen into line with reason, and that after all she was not the first to be deceived by 'this sad Prince'. One contemporary said that the foundation of the matter might have been 'anger or despite'.

Mary herself remarked that Darnley was 'the lustiest and best proportioned long man she had seen'. It is a physical appraisal rather than an avowal of love. Certainly Darnley proceeded with some caution on his coming to Mary's Court. 'His behaviour is well liked', wrote Randolph, 'and hitherto he so governs himself that there is great praise of him.' It was not to last long.

Soon the Queen began to show Darnley proofs of her favour, showering him with rich presents. In March 1565 she went to Stirling Castle, where Darnley followed her but immediately took to his bed with measles. It was an anti-climactic complaint for an ardent lover, but Mary nursed him with such devotion that some courtiers alleged she was already married. The English and Scottish Courts were seething with rumours.

Even the French were not pleased by Mary's lack of prudence. The Cardinal of Lorraine described Darnley as 'a pleasant hare-brain'.

But Mary was growing impatient, she had begun to realize that it was impossible to make a marriage to please the whole Renaissance world. Furthermore, she was young, and virtuous by religious training, and the role of a chaste young widow was becoming irksome.

Although Elizabeth had allowed Darnley to go to Scotland, it appeared she and her advisers were having second thoughts, for by April of 1565 Randolph had become alarmed: 'The Queen's familiarity with him breeds no small suspicions that there is more intended than merely giving him honour for his nobility.' The Scots lords were also displeased and openly spoke of her unprincely behaviour. 'They will shortly have it reformed' reports the English Ambassador 'or openly signify that what she has taken in hand tends to her own destruction and the overthrow of tranquillity of her realms—and must be helped by sharper means. They are not one or two, nor are they the meanest that speak it, nor the unlikeliest to execute it.' These remarks were a sombre presage of future events. Randolph goes on to say: 'She is now in utter contempt of her people, and so far in doubt of them herself that without speedy redress worse is to be feared.'

This has a ring of truth, of a woman determined to act in spite of everyone, with that febrile energy which action for the sake of action can bring. She had been waiting for so long for the right suitor, had been so often disappointed, that she was determined to settle the matter once and for all. This was the equivalent of the sudden, decisive reaction of her Guise uncles at Amboise which filled the Loire with floating bodies.

The Queen's favour rapidly turned Darnley's head and changed Randolph's fluctuating opinion of the young man. 'Woe that time that ever the Lord Darnley did set his foot in this country. This Queen in her love is so transported, and he is grown so proud that to all honest men he is intolerable, and almost forgetful of his duty to her already, that has adventured so much for his sake.' He adds sadly: 'What shall become of her?' In describing the fury of the Scots an ominous note sounds again: 'They find nothing but that God must send him a short end, or themselves a miserable life.' Was this a pious hope, or an inspired guess on the part of the sorely tried Ambassador, caught between Mary's determination to marry Darnley, and Elizabeth's anger at the idea of the marriage? In regard to Mary his genuine grief or disillusion shines through his words. He tells how altered she is, her beauty diminished, even her 'wits not what they were', adding that he pities her for she has no longer any regard for what is virtuous or good. 'How loathe I am thus to write, of her whom so many times and oft my chief delight has been always to set forth her worth equal to any I ever saw.' He adds, perhaps to give himself some cheer, that some people were of the opinion that Mary had been tainted by witchcraft.

When Mary's activities hardened into an iron determination to marry, Elizabeth had sent Throckmorton as a special envoy to her, in a last-minute attempt to delay things, but he reported: 'The Queen is so much decided on marriage with Darnley that the only means to stop the marriage is force.'

Whether as a result of this opinion, or whether the idea was suggested by the two Englishmen, towards the end of June Moray, Argyll and others held counsel at Lochleven, and told Randolph: 'whatever becomes of Darnley, he won't have a long life amongst this people.'

Shortly after this there were rumours of a plot to kidnap the Queen, possibly in an attempt to stop the marriage. On the 7 July, Cecil wrote in his journal: 'the bruit is abroad that the Queen of Scotland has been taken by the Earls of Moray and Argyll.'

The story is that the conspirators knew she was going to Callander to be godmother to the child of Lord Livingston. The way lay across a wild country, and although her brother Moray was to have accompanied her, he cried off. Mary herself believed in the plot and to thwart it made one of her dashing exits at five o'clock in the morning. Escorted by two or three hundred loyal gentlemen, she rode without a check the thirty miles which separate Perth from Callander, arriving at the hour when the conspirators believed she was setting out.

Whether there was a plot or not, Mary was in haste to be wedded and bedded. They may or may not have been secretly married, as some alleged, with Riccio, her *valet de chambre* turned secretary, producing a Friar Lawrence, but this story has a tang of nineteenth-century romantic revival about it. The banns were published on the 22 July, and on the same day Darnley was made Duke of Albany.

> At nine hours at night, by three heralds at the sound of the trumpet, he was proclaimed King. This was the night before the marriage. This day, Monday at twelve of the clock, the Lords, all that were in this town, were present at the proclaiming of him again, when no man said so much as 'amen' saving his father that cried out aloud 'God save his Grace'.
>
> Upon Sunday in the morning, between five and six, she was conveyed by divers of her nobles to the Chapel. She had upon her back the great mourning gown of black with the great wide mourning hood, not unlike unto that she wore the doleful day of the burial of her husband.
>
> The words were spoken, the rings which were three—the middle one a rich diamond—were put upon her finger, they knelt together, and many prayers were said over them he taketh a kiss and leaveth her there.

Darnley went out of the chapel after the nuptial blessing, and Mary heard Mass alone. It was a prudent move on Darnley's part to please the Protestants. After Mass she rejoined Darnley in her chamber, Randolph goes on to describe the change from grave to gay:

> according to the solemnity to cast off her care, and lay aside those sorrowful garments, and give herself to a pleasanter life. After some pretty refusal, more I believe for manner sake than grief of heart, she suffereth them that stood by, every man that could approach her to take out a pin, and so being committed unto her ladies, changed her garments, but went not to bed to signify unto the world that it was not lust moved them to marry, but only the necessity of her country, not if she will to leave it destitute of an heir.

Mary always had a sense of form, and in spite of her hasty actions before the ceremony, the marriage itself seems to have been managed with finesse. But even Mary's reluctance to be bedded did not stop the rumours, for Randolph mentions that suspicious men still supposed the married pair were already lovers, although he adds: 'The likelihoods are so great to the contrary that if it were possible to see such an act done, I would not believe it.'

After the marriage there was wine and dancing, and the nobles followed Mary and Darnley to dinner. 'The trumpets sound, a largesse cried, and money thrown about the house in great abundance to such as were happy to get any great part. Some dancing there was and so they go to bed.' The

English Ambassador says, and there is a touch of regret in the words: 'I was sent for to have been at the supper, but like a churlish or discourteous carl, I refused to be there.' It would have been imprudent to appear at the marriage.

Chapter IX

19. *Bothwell Castle* (Mansell Collection)

Destiny is woven of interconflicting threads of character and circumstances, and if Mary's marriage to Darnley was one of her major imprudences, her recall of Bothwell was equally fraught with disaster.

Darnley's arrogance, both before and after the marriage, had totally alienated Moray and his supporters who imprudently expressed their view that a King had been imposed upon them without consent of Parliament. She was married in late July and on the 1 August she summoned Moray and his accomplices to appear before her at Dumbarton Castle under pain of treason. No one obeyed. They were all 'put to the horn', that is, declared outlaws. The Queen then appointed Bothwell as Lieutenant of the Forces.

She had always shown a certain leniency towards his various and complicated escapades. Possibly this was because of his support of her mother, the Queen Dowager, or maybe because her very feminine character, with its strong streak of admiration for adventure, was drawn to his ruthlessness. Mary's mother had sent Bothwell as her envoy to France. While he was abroad, Marie de Guise died, and he had taken a passing opportunity to marry a Norwegian heiress, Anne Thorssen. Her fortune was said to be 40,000 yoendallers, which he apparently kept, while abandoning the lady. Throckmorton described Bothwell as a 'proud, rash and hazardous young man, his adversaries should have an eye to him'. It was unfortunate for Mary that she should not have taken the same detached view. The English Ambassador's opinion was that her reason for the appointment was because 'he bears an evil will against Moray'. His opinion of Bothwell was not flattering: 'He was a fit man to be minister to a shameful act be it either against God or man.' Bothwell's alleged remark that the two rival Queens 'could not make one honest woman' did not reflect a romantic view of either of them, but he had courage, resource, and feeling for quick action. In this Bothwell's character accorded with the Queen's needs of the moment. It also suited Mary's own liking for action, for forced marches, for adventure, and for sudden decisions.

The rebel lords, led by Moray, sent hurried messages to Elizabeth for help. But the English Queen, slow mover and double thinker, was not to be drawn into openly helping rebels against an anointed sovereign. Illicit funds were one thing, but open acts of war were another. Mary was already gathering her followers, for she was now fixed in an implacable desire to crush Moray, who had flouted her dignity as sovereign and who disapproved of her sudden marriage.

In a conversation with Randolph over her negotiations with Elizabeth, and with the rebels, the Queen referred, as always, to her rights and those of her husband. The English Embassador with sad irony remarked that he knew nothing about the question of rights, he had never examined them, but one thing he did know was that she was taking the quickest road to losing them, both for herself and for her husband. It was a flash of insight, a piece of horse sense given to a woman passionately and wrong-headedly determined on action.

On the 25 August 1565, a month after her marriage, Mary rode with her troops against the rebels. The campaign was arduous, the country wild, and the weather appalling. On the march, the army encountered a violent storm, so violent that burns were turned into torrents, and men, battered in the face by wind and rain, advanced only with difficulty. The Queen, always in the van, was for long hours in the saddle, in spite of the fury of the storm and the muddy ways. 'Her courage, energy, and indefatigable activity astonished her companions, and when she was reproached that she paid too little attention to her health, she laughingly replied "I will not rest until I have led you into London"', perhaps hardly the reply of a woman who wished no harm to her 'dear sister' and only asked to be left in peace in her rugged domain. Rumours that Mary wore a helmet and carried arms during the campaign so astonished Randolph that he refused to believe them. This was one aspect of Mary's character which the Ambassador had never seen.

The rebels, finding their allies not so numerous as they had sanguinely hoped, wrote to Mary offering their submission if she would restore their lands and dignities. Even the French Ambassador, who had arrived to congratulate her on her marriage, suggested compromise. The Queen replied that she was not to be dictated to by mere subjects. 'What they wished was to reign in her place, her spirit was too great to permit her kingdom to be converted into a republic.' With tears in her eyes she appealed to the French envoy for help from France, for she would rather lose an arm than think traitors had received any encouragement from France. Again the French Ambassador suggested the advantages of compromise. She replied: 'Rather would I languish and not be Queen.' Fate was to take her words literally.

The campaign against the rebels continued. There was much marching and counter-marching, and eventually the rebel lords fled over the Border into England.

With Mary's victory, opinions on the Continent changed. No longer were they urging compromise, they had now become firmly attached to the idea that the whole revolt had been due to Elizabeth's intrigues. Ignoring Mary's errors of judgement towards her difficult Scottish subjects, the *débâcle* was now due to perfidious Albion, and her even more perfidious Queen.

Elizabeth herself was not pleased at the outcome. She, who was so economical with her funds, had been supplying them to the losing side. She sent messages to the rebels giving her conditions. If they made public amends for their revolt against their sovereign, she would continue to help them privately. To this the rebels had perforce to agree, and the apologies were made before Elizabeth and a carefully staged assembly of foreign ambassadors. Moreover, for the benefit of the Ambassador, and to the further discomfort of the rebels, the apologies were required to be made in their execrable French.

Mary had temporarily gained the upper hand against her rebels, but the discontents remained, and chief amongst them was Riccio, her French secretary, who had come to the Court in the train of the Count de Morette, Ambassador of the Duke of Savoy. To the Scots, Riccio the Piedmontese was just one more foreigner whom they had to stomach, a deformed dwarf, who was a minion and tool of the Pope. Some historians say that the Scots' hatred of Riccio sprang from the fact that although he was low born and a foreigner, he showed himself to be more cultured than the local nobility. He had begun his Court life as a *valet de chambre*, engaged because of his sweet voice, with other singers, perfumers, tailors, and musicians dedicated to the cause of that 'fiddling and flinging' of which John Knox so disapproved.

He soon advanced in Mary's favour, and in the disfavour of the Scots, and became her confidential French secretary. Some accounts say that Riccio 'showed himself well-fitted for his new functions, most of the affairs of the kingdom passed through his hands, he conducted himself in all things with so much prudence'. But Melville told the Queen that Riccio should show himself more modest, and warned her that the Lords were offended when on entering her private apartments, they found her *tête à tête* with Signor Davie.

However, Mary had need of confidantes. She trusted Riccio and was not at all disposed to sacrifice him to the caprice of her lords. Her thoughts on the subject were: 'Should not a Prince dare delegate authority to a man of poor estate and raise him up? Should the great ones who already have power wish for more?' The sentiment was an echo of her childhood lessons. A prince was not as other men. His to propose and dispose, to elevate or to destroy. But the picture presented is of a small group of French-speaking courtiers in the centre of the dark Holyrood Palace surrounded by the vengeful Scottish nobles. The contemptuous words 'Little France' are still attached to the approaches of Mary's favourite place, Craigmillar Castle, as an echo of old jealousies.

Riccio may have conducted himself in some things with prudence, but fostering the Darnley marriage he had shown himself less than wise. Scarcely had ambassadorial congratulations been exchanged than the hymeneal bliss was over.

The truth of the break-up is difficult to piece together. Some writers take the view that Mary had felt a sudden sexual passion for Darnley, and then rejected him having found him wanting; others on the contrary feel that her nature was cold, and that the marriage bed meant nothing to her, and that having become pregnant she had achieved her object—an heir.

It is certain that Darnley neglected her, and became arrogant and impossible.

He gave himself up to hunting and hawking, or ran about the brothels of the town with other libertines of similar tastes. One writer says: 'M. de la Roi-Paussay arrived yesterday at Berwick, he is ill because Darnley had made him drunk with acqua composita.' A French historian notes that this was possibly 'whisky, the national liqueur'. That Darnley was drinking was certain. He insulted the Queen and spoke to her in such terms in front of others that she left the dinner table in tears. It was not a happy background.

To Darnley's depravity were added his ambition, and determination to have equal rights with Mary—the crown matrimonial—and this she refused to give him. In spite of this Darnley was giving orders without the Queen's knowledge. 'She takes it badly, seeing that he was giving an ear to her enemies, and forbade Riccio to seal any paper until she had already signed them.'

In an atmosphere of dissension and a country of faction there were not wanting subtle voices to inflame Darnley. Morton, one day to be Regent, put it succinctly: 'It was against nature that the hen should crow before the cock.' A debauched prince was good material for ambitious men anxious for change. A foreigner, a simple secretary, was governing in his place. How could Darnley obtain the crown matrimonial when the Queen had counsellors such as Bothwell and Huntly, or as long as Riccio held his influence over the Queen?

But Mary clung to her devoted Italian servant. He amused and distracted her with chess, with cards, and with music. Possibly he brought back to her the happy souvenirs of the lost gaiety of France. Holyrood held *longueurs* as well as menace. Riccio stayed closeted with her in her private apartments, and with the closed doors, the rumours against her honour spread. There were even hints that Moray's hatred of Mary was for reasons which were too shameful to set down on paper. All the inflammable material was there ready to the hands of the conspirators. From the passions, the plots and counter-plots, the evil shape of the conspiracy grew.

Two bonds were sealed, to put Riccio to death.

One bond was signed by the conspirators themselves, and the other by Darnley alone.

> We, Henry, by Grace of God, King of Scotland, and husband to the Queen's Majesty, for so much we having consideration of the gentle and good nature, with many other good qualities in her . . . also think it great conscience to us that are her husband to suffer her to be abused or seduced by certain privy persons, wicked and ungodly, especially a stranger Italian called Davie . . . we have devised to take these privy persons and slay them wherever it happeneth.

This bond was demanded from Darnley because he insisted that the murder should be committed in the presence of the Queen. The cock was going to draw blood in the presence of the hen. The palace with its twisting staircases quivered with plots, with rumours. Riccio was warned by an astrologer to beware of the bastard. To Riccio the 'bastard' meant the banished Moray, safely out of Scotland, but the astrologer's warning was against George Douglas, son of the Earl of Angus, one of the chief conspirators, only too close at hand. Others told him to return to his own land. 'Words, nothing but words,' said Riccio; 'the Scots proclaim much, but their threats are not carried out.' The Queen was warned, but she was convinced that all these rumours were only set about to frighten her secretary, and asked him to continue to serve her.

The bonds were signed on the 1 March. Everything was now ready, the conspirators were assembled and resolved. The Queen in her Palace awaited the birth of her first child, while the conspirators outside awaited the moment to strike.

Chapter X

20. *Queen Mary's bedroom, Holyrood Palace* (Mansell Collection)

Where men are concerned in an act of violence there can be as many hidden motives as overt ones. Darnley may have seen himself partly as an outraged husband. Moray doubtless aided and abetted as an act of revenge against the sister who had temporarily defeated him. Others saw the proposed killing as a first step in coercing the Queen to their better advantage.

Riccio was certainly unpopular for obvious reasons, but his murder and the subsequent treatment of the Queen on the night of the crime were acts against the Queen's Majesty which portended more serious treason. There is no doubt that Mary saw them in this light.

The drama of the murderous and intimate supper party glows through the centuries. Mary was seated at table with her few intimates, Riccio, the Countess of Argyll, her half-sister, Robert Stuart, and Arthur Erskine, her Master of the Horse. They were attended by servants. This inner supper chamber is very small, only twelve feet by ten, and of irregular shape. It is difficult to visualize five or six people wearing their rich costumes, being served by servants, in so small a space. Riccio had been singing, and had sat down at the table. He wore a damask robe, trimmed with fur, with a doublet of satin and velvet breeches; his cap was on his head. This attire was a symbol of the magnificence which he had attained by the Queen's favour. Each century has a symbol which lifts a man from the herd. The Renaissance chose richly jewelled and furred robes and chains of gold to differentiate the men who had arrived from the home-spun masses.

As the sounds of music were stilled in the inner room, the Palace was surrounded, and the courtyard filled with Morton's men.

The curtain which divided the inner room from the Queen's bedroom was quietly lifted and Darnley came in. The Queen asked if he had already supped, and he replied that he had supped early because knowing that she had retired to her apartments he feared that she might be indisposed. The echoes of the polite, cold *niaiseries* of estranged husband and wife echo down the years. He put an arm round his wife and kissed her. As he did so, Ruthven, gaunt and white, dressed in black armour, stood in the doorway. He had risen from his sick bed as if the smell of new blood might restore his ebbing strength. Mary, alarmed, still retained her iron courtesy and asked was Ruthven not sick.

'It is true that I was sick, but I am come to render you a service,' he said.

'What service can you render me at this moment?' asked the Queen.

Ruthven's fevered eyes looked directly at Riccio.

'To rid you of the villain who is at the end of the table, and who merits neither place, nor honour. We will not be governed by a varlet.'

The room and the bedroom beyond were now filled with armed men. From the candlelight and the singing, the scene changed to the clang of arms and armour. Like many accounts of sudden death, the murder of Riccio has become confused. Some describe the sudden entry of the con-spirators, the fear of Riccio who sprang up in terror and overturned the table, while Lady Argyll snatched a solitary candle from it as it fell. Mary's own account said that the table was deliberately overturned and that she herself felt a pistol held to her womb, and the touch of the steel daggers as they struck Riccio. Some deny that the Italian was stabbed in the Queen's presence, but all agree that in the darkness and the tumult, Riccio clung to the Queen crying: 'Madame, sauvez ma vie, sauvez ma vie!'

Other accounts say that a pistol was pointed at the Queen, but that it failed to go off, and that the Queen cried: 'Fire, if you have no care for the child I carry in my womb.' This sentiment sounds too histrionically conventional for a pregnant woman, with an hysterical man clinging to her skirts, in semi-darkness, with a press of armed men around her.

Darnley held his wife, and prevented her from defending her servant. Riccio's fingers were bent back until he relaxed his grip, and he was dragged away uttering shrieks and cries for mercy. The wretched secretary was then killed in the Queen's bedroom. His body was stabbed fifty-six times. Fawdonside had struck the first of these blows. One of the con-spirators then came back into the supper room and took Darnley's dagger. This was the last stroke to enter Riccio's body, and made sure of the King's complicity.

'Davie was hurled down the steps of the stairs from the place where he was slain and brought to the porter's lodge; where the porter's servant, taking off his clothes, said that this was his destiny, for upon this chest was his first bed when he entered his place.'

When the death of Riccio was reported to Mary, accounts of her words vary. Some say they were: 'Poor faithful Davie,' others that she said: 'No more tears, I will think upon a revenge.' It is possible that she expressed both sentiments, for they showed the two sides of her character.

Even with the background of murder, the hands stained with blood, the treachery, and the courtyard filled with armed men, the reproaches of husband and wife confronting one another were simple and ordinary. Six months before the wife had been accustomed to come to his chamber, Darnley said, and how she was closeted away from him. She had denied him his marriage rights, while she played cards and amused herself with the dead Riccio. Feebly Darnley asked why he had become the object of her contempt. She answered that she wished no longer to live with him as his wife.

The tocsin sounded over the town, and the townspeople came clamouring to the Palace to know what was amiss. The Queen wished to show herself to the people, but the conspirators, fearing some support for her, and possibly not certain of some of their fellow conspirators, would not allow her to appear. She was threatened that if she did appear she would be 'cut into collops'. If Mary wrote that the Scottish nobility lacked manners, she was not proved wrong on the night of the murder. Eventually Darnley appeared at the window to reassure the waiting townspeople of the Queen's safety.

Bothwell, Huntly, and Atholl, alarmed by the tocsin and the tumult, attempted to come to the Queen's rescue, but the conspirators had the Palace firmly in their grip. Bothwell and his allies escaped 'through a little window where the lions were lodged'.

Mary was now without any means of defence, and she was locked up alone for the night. A pregnant woman at the mercy of her enemies, she might seem to be without resources, but to the subtle mind, even pregnancy can be turned to advantage. She decided on a ruse. The following morning, when Darnley came to her, she was sweetness itself. The foolish young man was soon convinced that she believed in his innocence, and in his protestation that he had no part in the murder or the conspiracy. Whether she did believe it is doubtful. But her charm, and her apparent weakness, drew him to her, and she extracted from him the names of the conspirators.

Later that day, she feigned illness. In view of the night's happenings and her advanced pregnancy it would not have been unlikely for her to have been taken ill. Darnley, perhaps afraid for her life, or his own reputation, sent for the midwife and her French doctor. They insisted that she must be removed from her close confinement. The guards were removed from her doors so that her ladies and servants could come and go.

When her brother, Moray, came to her in the evening she affected a reconciliation with him. Weeping, she said that had he been in the Palace, she would never have been subjected to such indignities. Whether at this moment the two deceivers, both wishing for more real power and conscious of their rights, were deceived in one another can be questioned. Subsequently the other lords also came to her, and as they knelt before her she forgave them. The floor of the Queen's chamber was still stained with Riccio's blood, but Morton, pin-pointing the reason for the murder, said that the death of one mean man was not important, what was more important was the ruin of 'many noble lords'. That the lords had given little indication of nobility the previous night was of no consequence.

The lords then withdrew to the house of the Earl of Morton to debate the success of their plot, but not without misgivings. They did not trust Mary with Darnley. Her charm could lead him 'to follow her will and desire, by reason she hath been trained up from her youth in the Court of France'. Treachery was one thing, but treachery against traitors was another.

They were right to be uneasy. As soon as they had left, Mary's aspect changed. In a few minutes, she was transformed from a suffering female about to miscarry, into a Queen ready for action. She ordered horses, commanded Darnley to follow her, and made her way out through the Palace kitchen, past her French chefs and pastrycooks, through the graveyard of the Abbey, past the newly dug grave of Riccio. She was free.

Mounted behind Erskine, with five other riders including Darnley, she rode through the night to Dunbar Castle, the rocky fortress bounded on two sides by the sea which washes at its feet. Here she found Bothwell. He immediately set off to raise an army for her defence, and returned to the Castle at the head of a force of fighting men. Their numbers are variously given as twelve hundred to four thousand. When the news of Mary's army spread, two of the rebel earls immediately came to the Castle and surrendered. The others fled to England. Even John Knox felt it judicious to retreat to Ayrshire and to preserve his thunderbolts at a safe distance.

Mary rode back into Edinburgh at the head of her troops. Although heavily pregnant, after only five days she was again victorious, and had regained control of her country and her vacillating husband. For when Darnley heard of the flight of his accomplices he merely remarked: 'As they have brewen so let them drink.' He felt assured that his change of allegiance had been unremarked, and that the bond had been buried with Riccio.

Mary had escaped her enemies, and the child in her body was still living. In addition, she had achieved the unification of the North and South by promoting the marriage of Bothwell to Huntly's sister, Janet. Huntly and Bothwell were the two men whom she trusted. But political wisdom is often counterbalanced by human emotion, and the consequences of Bothwell's wise political marriage were yet to come.

Darnley immediately laboured to re-instate himself in the favour of the populace and issued a proclamation professing his non-involvement in the murder plot: 'For as much as divers seditious and wicked persons have maliciously spread rumours, bruits, and privy whisperings . . . slanderously and irreverently backbiting the King's majesty.' It ended, and this is the simple, sincere and plain truth.' A contemporary says, 'Proclamation was made by a herauld, and that not without laughter'.

Before the birth of her son, Mary managed to reconcile the warring lords, and even induced Huntly and Bothwell to make peace with Moray. Lethington came back into her favour, and outwardly her differences with Darnley were patched up. For the birth of the child was now imminent, and she was anxious to secure the succession. Whatever her feelings for Darnley, like the Frenchwoman she was, her child was to be protected, and for this reason, in the will she made before the birth, her husband was mentioned with affection. Personal feelings were one thing, the succession was another.

The child was born in Edinburgh Castle on the 19 June 1566. Shortly after the birth Darnley went in to her. She said: 'My lord, God has given you and me a son begotten by none but you. This is your son, and no other man's son. And I am desirous that all here, with ladies and others, bear witness.' Then she went on: 'This is the son who, I hope, shall first unite the two kingdoms of Scotland and England.' When asked why the son should succeed before herself and Darnley she said: 'Because his father has broken to me.'

Darnley asked if this was the forgiving and forgetting of which she had spoken, and his wife replied: 'I have forgiven all, but will never forget.'

She then asked what would have become of her and the child if Fawdonside's pistol had been discharged. The memories of the murder night were still in her mind, and the suspicion remained that the attempt was as much against herself and the coming child as against Riccio.

The birth was celebrated by bonfires and the ringing of bells by the populace, who, as always, felt that their troubles were at an end. Messengers were sent post-haste to bring the news of the birth to Elizabeth, who received it with a sudden gloom. Her stock was barren, she said, but the Queen of Scotland was lighter of a fair son. But the following morning Queen Elizabeth managed to give the impression of 'sisterly' happiness, and even consented to be the child's godmother.

As soon as Mary had recovered from her confinement, she set off on a journey to Alloa, a journey which has been variously construed. Buchanan says: 'The Queen left her favour to the Earl of Bothwell, with one or two attendants passed down to Newhaven without letting any mortal know whither she was hurrying,' and goes on to say that Bothwell's crew were pirates, and that in Alloa Castle 'where the ship arrived, she demeaned herself for some days, as if she had forgot not only royal dignity, but even the modesty of matron'.

Whether the Queen did at this time feel drawn to Bothwell in a physical way is an open question. He was her saviour, and it would not have been surprising if she had felt some gratitude and affection for him. The sources of her support were frail and fraught with danger, but in an age when loss of chastity was avenged with a knife edge, even a Queen would not so lightly and publicly throw it away. The other point which militates against this honeymoon with pirates is that she was still politically trying to paper over her open differences with Darnley.

Her overriding pride could have led her at this point to an open break with her husband. But politically it was inexpedient for the legitimacy of her son that this should happen. She again attempted reconciliation. Randolph, the ever-present reporter, writes: 'I have heard that since Mauvissière's going there, the King and Queen are bedded together whereby 'tis thought some better agreement may ensue'. Possibly advice from her compatriot had convinced Mary that charm and wifely affection might achieve something which opposition could destroy. She had cajoled him once when her life was threatened, and to good effect.

But Darnley was still not satisfied; he craved the power for which he was not fitted. If he did not receive the crown matrimonial, he threatened to leave for France, although later when publicly questioned by the French Ambassador, Du Croc, he could give no specific reason for his discontents. Unwilling, or perhaps unable, to substantiate his grievances, he made a childish exit saying: 'Adieu, Madame, you shall not see my face for a long while.'

The influence of Darnley grew less with the Queen, and with his former allies, but Bothwell's power was growing. The Queen had appointed him Lieutenant General of the Marches, and had re-instated him as Lord High Admiral. His riches grew apace with his influence and he was seizing the sources of power.

In October he was wounded in a border affray when he 'went before to bring in some of the Elliotts, a small unruly tribe, living near the borders. Accordingly one of them assaulted him unawares, whom, it seems, he slew, but not until he himself was first grievously wounded'. Mary's reaction to the wounding of Bothwell was to ride from Jedburgh immediately, thirty miles and back in one day.

Admittedly a Queen would be naturally concerned for the health of her chief military adviser, but normally Heads of States are not concerned to ride post-haste themselves to the scene of disasters to their staff, they leave the physical effort to others, and content themselves with mental worry. This ride is, on the other hand, the natural reaction of a woman in the mounting grip of sexual attraction, a woman who must see the loved object in order to reassure herself on his safety.

When she returned to Jedburgh from the Hermitage where Bothwell lay: 'She was so far affected by the night air, she was seized with a malignant fever, and lay as if she had been quite dead, then falling into a great sweat the fever left her.' The threads of mental states and physical

James VI and I, attributed to Arnold Bronkhorst (Scottish National Portrait Gallery)

Mary, Queen of Scots in secondary mourning, artist unknown (Scottish National Portrait Gallery)

manifestations are very close, and many illnesses can be traced to spiritual unease.

Buchanan, ever ready to weigh in with elaborations to Mary's discredit, says:

> While the Queen and Bothwell were yet both sick, she of the fever and he of his wound, she in great feebleness of her body, paid him visits every day. And when both begin to be a little better, but before they had sufficiently recovered strength, they returned to their wonted pastime, and so publicly too that they seemed to dread nothing more than that their lewdness should be unknown.

The Queen's view of Buchanan was more succinct: 'Buchanan is known to be a lewd man and an atheist.'

21. *George Buchanan* (Scottish National Portrait Gallery)

Chapter XI

But there is no prudence below the girdle.
LORD EGMONT

22. LEFT: *Casket showing the lock and key* (The Duke of Hamilton)

23. RIGHT: *Front of casket showing place whence the lock has been 'stricken up'* (The Duke of Hamilton)

The future James I was baptized on the 17 December 1566, and on the 9 February of the following year his father was killed. Between those two dates, the fate of Mary was unknowingly decided by Bothwell.

It was not until the 20 November that Darnley rejoined Mary at Craigmillar Castle. After this visit, Mary again became ill, and fell into another profound depression. 'The Queen is in the hands of the Doctors', says Du Croc, 'and I think the principal cause of her malady is a great grief which it is not possible for her to forget, she often repeats that she wishes she were dead.'

The French Ambassador then recounts an interview with Darnley, and says that things are going from bad to worse. 'But I am assured that he [Darnley] will not take part in the Baptism. I do not expect any reconciliation unless God take a good hand in it.'

At Craigmillar there was some discussion of Mary's divorce from Darnley. Those concerned in it were Moray, Lethington, and Argyll. Their objects were to secure the Queen's consent to a divorce, and to engineer the return of the exiled Morton and his supporters. 'Do not be disquieted,' said Lethington, 'we will find the means of ridding her of her husband, so long as you and Lord Huntly lend us your support.' Moray and Lethington called Huntly, and promised him help in the return of part of his estates. The five conspirators, who included Bothwell, then went to find the Queen.

Lethington was their spokesman. He recalled the numerous offences of the King, and said that if the Queen would pardon Morton and his companions she would find the means of procuring a divorce without having to concern herself in it. But she must decide promptly because, if Darnley remained her husband, as King he would not rest until he had done her an ill turn for which it would be impossible to find a remedy. But the Queen would not consent to the idea of divorce unless it was in accordance with the law, and would in no way affect the rights of her son, 'otherwise she was resolved to endure all torments, and brave all dangers'.

Bothwell observed that divorce would not prejudice the child's rights, for he himself was the child of divorced parents, and had inherited the estates and dignities of his father. As an augury Bothwell was not a happy example.

Mary seemed undecided; she might separate from Darnley, on the other hand he might repent of his errors, or perhaps she would return to France for a space. Lethington soothed her, she must not be alarmed for 'we shall find the means that your Majesty shall be quit of him without hurt to your son. And albeit that my lord Moray here present be little less scrupulous for a Protestant than your Grace is for a Papist, I am assured he will look through his fingers, and will behold our doings, saying nothing to the same.'

Mary replied: 'I will that ye do nothing through which any spot may be laid upon mine honour or conscience, and therefore I pray you, rather let the matter be, lest your believing that you are doing me a service may possibly turn to my hurt any displeasure.'

The results of the meeting at Craigmillar were inconclusive. She wanted to be rid of her husband. There were close by her at Craigmillar men of similar mind. Yet between the wish for freedom and the deed to be done lay a gulf. A gulf which remains a mystery and a question mark.

The idea of divorce was dropped, and in December Mary went to Stirling Castle for the christening of her son. Darnley was lodged in a house apart, and Mary in the castle itself where her melancholy was remarked. 'She was sad and pensive and sighed heavily, though few sought to console her.'

In spite of the grand company, the representatives of the King of France, the Queen of England, the Duke of Savoy, the baby's cloth of gold, the splendid velvets and brocades of the nobles, and even the gold baptismal font sent by Queen Elizabeth, his godmother, the cracks in the fabric of the State were again becoming apparent. Darnley was still sulking, and his refusal to appear at the baptismal ceremony was yet another attempt to brand his son a bastard.

The French Ambassador wrote:

She conducted herself admirably during the whole of the Baptismal ceremony, and went to the greatest pains to treat all the brave assembly well, which made her forget her cares for an instant. But I am of the opinion nevertheless that she will cause us some anxiety, and I cannot think otherwise as long as she continues to be so sad and melancholy. She sent for me yesterday, and I found her on her bed crying bitterly. She complained of a pain in her side. I am afflicted to see her exposed to so many troubles and setbacks.

The Frenchman was uneasy. He could see the signs of a woman who was losing control, both of herself and of the situation, and indeed with slow inevitability the tragedy moved forwards. Darnley departed to Glasgow where he felt, no doubt, that he would be protected amongst his father's people.

The sequence of events leading up to the murder of Darnley is not difficult to set down. Mary went to Glasgow in January 1567, returning with the ailing Darnley in a litter, and on the night of the 9/10 February he was killed. Mary's complicity in the matter rests on the authenticity of what are known as the 'Casket Letters', which were supposedly written to Bothwell, and conveyed to him by Nicolas Hubert, nicknamed French Paris, his body-servant.

The letters themselves read as a sombre page of a play about the interplay of adultery, treachery, and murder. It would be difficult for a man, even the most expert of forgers, to imagine the mind of a woman in such complicated detail.

A strong, newly aroused sexual passion is ruthless, is humble, and disregards the man to be destroyed, for he has become a mere object in the way of the fulfilment of the desire. The fact that once the object is achieved it becomes illusory does not mitigate the enduring strength and destructiveness of the urge while it lasts. A woman like Mary, brought up to be admired, adulated, clever, charming, and tricky, would be more, not less, foolhardy in the grip of a primitive force which she had not experienced so fully before. Up to the time of her passion for Bothwell she had been protected from the full folly of her sexual nature. Whether, as she alleged, Bothwell had raped her, and that her subsequent marriage to him had been to regularize the situation, has little bearing on the fact that she married her husband's murderer. Mary Stuart considered herself above the ordinary run of men and women. She was a 'Prince' and felt herself to be outside the law of the land. It was the law of nature which defeated her.

The Casket Letters supposedly written by Mary to Bothwell are the hinge on which rests her guilt or innocence. These letters breathe pride in her passion, with little compassion for the man she was possibly luring to his death. 'He is the merriest that ever you saw, and doth remember unto me all that he can, to make me believe that he loveth me. To conclude you would say that he maketh love to me, wherein I take so much pleasure that I have never come in there.' The discarded husband is always a comic figure, whether in farce or tragedy.

'Being gone from the place where I had left my heart it may be easily judged what my countenance was considering what the body without heart, which was the cause that till dinner I had used little talk, neither would anybody venture himself thereunto, thinking it was not good so to do.' This is the silence and self-absorption of a woman wrapped in her own passion.

The letter writer then goes on to explain in detail a long conversation in which Darnley gives proofs of his returning love for her, his desire to reform, of her cross-questioning him about his going to France.

> He would not let me go. I made as though all to be true, and that I would think upon it, and have excused myself from sitting up with him this night.
>
> You have never heard him speak better nor more humbly, and if I had not proof of his heart to be as wax and that mine were not as diamond, no stroke but coming from your hand would make me but to have pitie of him. But fear not the place shall contine till death . . . He hath almost told me all . . . I have taken the worms out of his nose [i.e. drawn the truth from him], God knit us together for ever for the most faithful couple that ever he did knit together. This is my faith; I will die in it.
>
> Excuse it if I write ill, you must guess the other half I cannot do with all, for I am ill at ease and glad to write unto you when other folk be asleep, seeing that I cannot do as they do, according to my desire, that is between your arms my dear life whom I beseech God to preserve from all ill.

Then from passion the writer returns to irritation with the human obstacle in its way.

> Cursed be this pocky fellow that troubles me thus much. I thought I should have been killed with his breath, for it is worse than your uncle's breath, and yet I was set no nearer to him than in a chair by his bolster, and he lieth at the further side of the bed. This day I have wrought till two of the clock upon this bracelet . . . but I will make a fairer, and in the mean time take heed that none of those that be here do see it, for all the world would know it, for I have made it in haste in their presence.

The simple desire to give presents and to please is common to every woman in the toils of love. One commentator says of this letter, 'a rustic wench trying painfully to write a letter would have succeeded better, it is a singular and incoherent jumble'. People in the grip of powerful emotions do express themselves badly. Birth, love, and death are primitive forces which can bring the lowly to the heights, and the powerful to the depths.

The letter goes on:

> You make me dissemble so much that I am afraid thereof with horror, and you make me almost play the part of a traitor. Remember that if it were not for obeying I had rather be dead. My heart bleedeth for it. To be short he will not come but with condition that I shall promise to be with him as heretofore at bed and board, and that I shall forsake him no more, and upon my word, he will do what I will, and will come but he hath prayed me to tarry till tomorrow.

Darnley's illness has been variously described as smallpox, or more likely, considering his symptoms, and predilection for the whorehouses of Edinburgh, syphilis. A weak man riddled with syphilis is doubtless an unattractive object, and for Mary, in her blindness of passion, it was not to be expected that Darnley would have roused more than a passing pity, speedily quenched.

Darnley was not without his suspicions. The writer goes on: 'And even touching the Lady Reres, he said "God grant that she serve your honour" . . . to conclude for a surety, he mistrusteth her of that you know, and for his life. But in the end, after I had spoken two or three good words to him, he was very merry and glad.' Lady Reres, a confidante of Mary's, was suspected of being a go-between for Mary and Bothwell. In this letter breathing adultery and treachery Lady Reres is mentioned in the same sentence as Darnley's fear of murder. If the writer did not consider the two things were interconnected why did they spring to mind in the same sentence? The letter makes clear that she was jealous of the lawful wife:

> See not also her whose feigned tears you ought not more to regard than those true travails which I endure to deserve her place, for obtaining of which, against my own nature, I do betray those that could let me. God forgive me, and give you, my only friend, the good luck and prosperity that your humble and faithful lover doth wish unto you, who hopeth shortly to be another thing unto you, for the reward of my pains.

Many writers dismiss the Casket Letters out of hand as forgeries because the original French versions no longer exist. Small discrepancies are enlarged as sure proofs of forgery. They have been said to be letters written to Bothwell by some other woman, into which incriminating sentences have been interpolated, or simply straight inventions of Mary's enemies.

Mary herself denied the authorship. 'I never writ anything concerning that matter to any creature. There are divers in Scotland, both men and women, that can counterfeit my handwriting.' But later in her life, she denied writing the letters concerned in the Babington plot, and the authenticity of these is not in doubt.

When the Casket Letters were published to the world in 1571, she kept silence, and her friends kept silence. When versions of the letters, and a copy of Buchanan's scurrilous book against her, were sent to her by Elizabeth, she denounced the book. The letters she did not mention. There may be no prudence below the girdle, but once prudence has returned the written proof of passion is merely embarrassing.

When Darnley was brought back to Edinburgh by Mary, there was talk of his being taken to Craigmillar Castle, as being more inducive to his recovery. In the event he was lodged in a house in Kirk o'Field. This is variously described as being a delightful house with a pleasant garden, or by other writers as in a dubious part of the town, the house ruinous and falling to pieces. Mary's excuse for lodging him apart was that she was afraid that, being ill, he might give the infection to the infant Prince James. But she sent for furniture to make Darnley's lodging more comfortable, tapestries, a velvet chair, and a bed.

Many volumes have been written about the murder of Darnley, but John Knox's account is succinct.

The Queen resorted often to visit him, and lay in the house two nights by him, although her lodging was in the palace of Holyrood House. Every man marvelled at this reconciliation and sudden change. The 9th February the King was murdered, and the house where he lay burned with powder, about twelve o'clock at night. His body was cast forth into a yard without the town wall adjoining close by. There was a servant likewise murdered beside him, who had also been in the chamber with him. The people ran to behold the spectacle; and wondering thereat some judged one thing, some another.

And for the last four hundred years, they have been doing the same. Knox continued:

Shortly thereafter, Bothwell came from the Abbey with a company of men of war, and caused the body of the King to be carried to the next house; where after a little the chirugeons being convened at the Queen's command, to view and consider the manner of his death, most part gave out, to please the Queen, that he was blown up in the air, albeit he had no mark of fire; and truly he was strangled. Soon after, he was carried to the Abbey, and there buried.

No amount of facts about the inordinate amount of gunpowder used to blow up such a small house, the comings and goings of the cloaked conspirators, or that Mary at the time of the murder had left the house to dance at the wedding of one of her servants, can alter the account set down by John Knox.

The Frenchman, M. de Morette, who left Edinburgh thirty-six hours after the murder recounted various circumstances which could make the world believe that Mary had known or permitted the death of her husband. But when the Spanish Ambassador, de Silva, asked him his opinion, 'by what he had seen and reflected on. He did not condemn her, but he did not exonerate her either'. Like many Scottish murder cases, the verdict against Mary is, to date 'not proven'.

On receipt of the news Elizabeth immediately wrote a shocked letter to her fellow Queen. She was horrified and astounded at what she had heard, but said that she would not be doing the office of a faithful friend if she studied 'how to please your ears'. She went on to add that the general rumours were that 'you look through your fingers, and have no care to touch those who have done you such pleasure', and that the belief was that the murder would not have been done without its perpetrators being assured of their safety. Elizabeth did not mince her words or lose sight of essential facts.

Mary then went to Seton, where it was reported that she was reposing herself by shooting, as well as playing golf and pall mall with Bothwell, Lord Seton, and the Earl of Huntly. But by the beginning of March, she was in a darkened room hung with black, mourning Darnley in the same way as she had mourned François II.

The populace had no belief in this mourning. Bills were posted on the Tolbooth, with Bothwell's likeness on them, and underneath the words: 'Here is the murderer of the King.' Other broadsheets linked Mary with the murder. Bothwell, true to type, roamed the town accompanied by fifty armed followers, declaring that if 'he knew who were the setters up of the bills he would wash his hands in their blood'.

Mary spent some time writing letters full of complicated explanations to her friends and relations in Europe. In a letter to Archbishop Beaton in Paris she talks of the 'sudden mischief' which had happened to her husband, and in the same letter asks for the despatch of 40,000 francs which she urgently needed.

In spite of the explanations and the letters it was generally said that 'the judgement of the people is that the Queen will marry Bothwell'.

Chapter XII

25. *Edinburgh Castle, from the south-west (facsimile of a Dutch engraving from a drawing by Gordon of Rothiemay)* (Mansell Collection)

The public clamour caused by the murder of Darnley grew in volume. At first the Queen took no action against Bothwell, she procrastinated, while her public and private explanations were full of grateful thanks for her own escape from death. The certainty that the plot must have been directed against her person filled her letters to France. But the scandal sheets and the scandal grew, and at last public opinion forced her to hold an open trial of Bothwell. This was hurriedly fixed for the 12 April.

Elizabeth wrote urgently requesting Mary to defer it, so that more evidence could be gathered. 'For the love of God, Madam, use such sincerity and prudence in this case which touches you so closely, that the world will have reason to deliver you as innocent from so great a crime.'

But Mary was constitutionally devoid of either fundamental sincerity or natural prudence. She was a creature of sudden tears and rages, or courage in action, and charm and wit used for her own ends; of the patient waiting game, of which Elizabeth was supreme mistress, she would have none. In this case Elizabeth's call for prudence was useless, the letter arrived on the very day of the trial and did not even reach Mary. Bothwell sent word to the messenger that 'the Queen was yet sleeping' and had not time to read it. He had made his own arrangements.

The trial was held at the Tolbooth, and great throngs of citizens filled the streets around it. Bothwell 'passed with a merry and lusty cheer' attended by two hundred arquebusiers who 'kept the door that none might enter, but such as were more for one side than the other'. A man who turns up with two hundred armed men is more likely to be found not guilty than one who is unaccompanied. Bothwell was acquitted. Some historians say 'after due deliberation', others because he had packed the court with his supporters.

The Earl of Moray prudently left Scotland for England on his way to Italy, which he had developed a sudden desire to visit. He confided to the Spanish Ambassador in London that the real reason for his journey was that he was afraid of unpleasant occurrences of which he himself might be the victim. Bothwell had four thousand men at his disposal, besides all the artillery in Dunbar and Edinburgh Castles. Moray further added that he had no intention of staying in a country where 'so strange and extraordinary a crime went unpunished'.

He confirmed the news of the divorce of Bothwell from his wife, Janet. The Ambassador stated that he had heard it asserted in French circles as certain that the Queen would marry Bothwell, but Moray professed to be extremely shocked by the suggestion, 'considering her great virtue'.

In Edinburgh events were less clear. Parliament confirmed Bothwell's acquittal, and also his possession of the Castle of Dunbar 'for his great and manifold services'. Morton, Huntly, and Moray too were given grants of land. The Queen even formally recognized the Reformed Church, but all this evidence of goodwill did not dampen down popular feelings and outrage over the murder. A man walked up and down the streets of Edinburgh calling out: 'Lord open the heavens, and pour down vengeance on me and those that have destroyed innocent blood,' and although the crier of vengeance was gaoled, the rumours went unmolested.

On the night of his official 'cleansing' Bothwell gave a supper party at Ainslie's tavern at which he forced, or persuaded, many of the leading nobles to sign a bond promising to aid him, both against his accusers and in his plans to marry the Queen. The day following the supper party, Kirkcaldy of Grange wrote a letter saying that the Queen was 'so shamefully enamoured of Bothwell that she had been heard to say that she cared not to lose France, England, and her country for him, and will go with him to the world's end in a white petticoat rather than leave him'. In late April, Kirkcaldy again wrote predicting that not only was Mary going to marry Bothwell, but also that she would be abducted on her return from Stirling, that Bothwell had gathered a number of his armed friends for this purpose, and that it was then planned to take her to Dunbar Castle. He adds sarcastically, 'Judge ye if it be with her will or no!'

Events turned out exactly as predicted. When Mary rode back from Stirling she was met by Bothwell with a large force of horsemen, and carried off to Dunbar Castle. In her account of abduction, she states that her small party had attempted to defend her, but she had forbidden them to take up arms, saying 'that she was ready to go with the Earl of Bothwell wherever he wished rather than bloodshed and death should result'. This meekness of conduct was unusual in the Queen of Scots.

The happenings at Dunbar Castle are unknown. She herself implied in her messages to the French Court that she had been overcome by force. Others say that 'it was with the Queen's consent', or that 'the manner of Bothwell's meeting with the Queen, although it appeared to be forcibly is yet known to be otherwise'. Very few people believed the story of rape. Although Mary indulged in an extensive correspondence putting a reasonable face on the situation: 'Albeit we found his doings rude, yet were his answer and words but gentle.' Few people found such explanations credible.

Historians who believe in Mary's innocence picture her in the toils of a ruffian who raped her, or seduced her, compelling her to become the tool of his ambition. This does not entirely fit in with her subtle actions after the Riccio murder, nor her subsequent battles and courageous escapes. She was not a woman given to submission, except possibly in sudden physical passion.

A convenient divorce was arranged for Bothwell, it being suddenly discovered that he was a distant cousin of his wife's, and that therefore the marriage was invalid. For full measure, his wife accused him of adultery. This caused some surprise in an age when wives were expected to condone adultery in husbands, while keeping themselves chaste.

Mary returned to Edinburgh with Bothwell, and demanded of Craig, Knox's deputy, that he should marry them. But Craig refused. He was the only man to defy Bothwell, and this was no mean feat of will when the Earl held not only the Queen but the whole of the capital in his grip. The Queen repeated her demand for the celebration of the marriage by Craig, assuring him in writing of the fact that 'she was neither ravished nor yet retained in captivity'. Craig then gave way, but not before calling heaven to witness his abhorrence of the marriage, and accusing Bothwell of murder, rape, and illegal divorce. The Reformers may have been over-given to sermonizing, but they did not lack the courage of their convictions.

Mary created Bothwell Duke of Orkney, 'placing the coronet on his head with her own hands', and on the 15 May she married him according to the rites of the Reformed Church, wearing the same mourning she had affected at her first Scottish wedding.

On the day following the wedding the lovers were already at odds. The ubiquitous Du Croc reports that Mary said that if she were sad it was simply because 'she could not rejoice for she did nothing but wish for death'. He added for good measure that on her wedding day she screamed aloud, and called for a knife to stab herself. The careful ambassador went on to say that he had attempted to comfort Mary, but that quite frankly he would rather not have had any part of this marriage, and that if he had had his way he would have left Edinburgh before it had taken place.

Mary's attitude towards her marriage to Bothwell can be taken as proof of coercion, or merely that she repented of her bargain. Her contemporaries tell how Bothwell's suspicions caused her to 'shed abundance of salt tears', and indeed that she never ceased to wail and lament. They also speak of Bothwell's jealousy in not allowing her to look at or be looked on by anyone. Mary, on her side, was equally jealous, perhaps with reason, since it was said that Bothwell passed some nights a week with the wife he had divorced. If Mary was an accessory to the murder of her husband, this would account for the tears and the jealousies. She had endured much to attain fleshly delights.

It was remarked that although the newly married pair behaved in public like turtle doves, yet they never went out except when accompanied by armed men. Moreover the marriage had become an international scandal. The ambassadors, Papal Nuncios, and ex-friends of the Queen at various courts were exchanging the latest news and gossip. Her diplomatic friends fell away one by one. The Pope, incensed probably by her marrying in the Huguenot rite, gave up her cause. Others said the reason for her hurried marriage was that she was pregnant. Even Mary's Dominican confessor left her. He was not entirely satisfied that her marriage had been, as she said, 'to settle religion by that means'. For a convinced Catholic, it was certainly a thin excuse.

Queen Elizabeth was in two minds about Mary's pending downfall. While the Scottish Queen's disgrace was a blow to Catholic hopes, the English Queen was not convinced that any queen's downfall was good for monarchies in general.

In Scotland the lords now gathered against the Queen and Bothwell, sending word that unless she dismissed her soldiers, and Bothwell, they would not obey her. She was also refused permission to see her child, if she should bring Bothwell with her, for the heir, Prince James, had already become another pawn in the power game.

Mary and Bothwell set about rallying their forces, and as armies need paying, the Queen's plate, and even the gold christening font, were melted down to make gold pieces for this purpose. A contemporary writes: 'One has told me that he saw the font broken, and also upon Wednesday the Queen bitterly wept.' The Queen's supporters were not only short of funds but at odds. On one occasion Bothwell tried to kill Lethington, and would have succeeded but for the Queen's intervention. Lethington, foreseeing the downward trend in the Queen's fortunes, escaped from her entourage, and made his way to join the forces of the rebel lords. Moreover, and ominously, the levies were not flocking to the standard of the Queen while she remained at Bothwell's side.

The lords then marched on Borthwick Castle where the Queen and Bothwell were being besieged by a thousand men led by the Earl of Morton and Lord Home. It must have been a loose, ramshackle siege for both Bothwell and Mary escaped, the latter in man's clothing, booted and spurred.

Eventually they managed to muster an army, and with slow inevitability the lords moved against them. The two opposing forces met at Carberry Hill. The French Ambassador, Du Croc, while politely refusing to join in

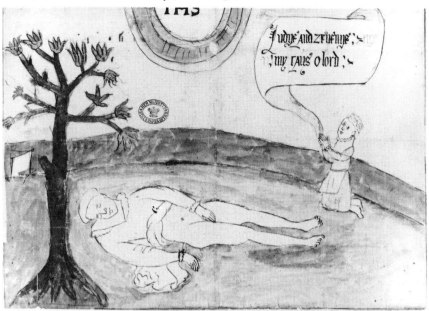

the fight, followed the army of the lords with his own modest ten horse-men, having the intention of acting as mediator.

While the two armies waited, confronting one another, accusations and counter-accusations were delivered. Even in her danger Mary was in-transigent, throwing the lords' accusations back at them. They themselves had married her to Bothwell whom they now accused. She declared, with some audacity, that if they would acknowledge their fault and ask her pardon, she was ready to open her arms and embrace them. Bothwell was equally uncompromising, sarcastically demanding to know if he was the man the lords wanted. He taunted them, saying 'that there was not one of them who would not like to be in his place'.

The banner under which the lords' army marched made their position quite clear. It was a white ensign on which there was a dead man near a tree, and a child on its knees, representing the Prince James. Underneath were written the words: 'Judge and Revenge my Cause, O Lord.'

In spite of their warlike array, the opposing armies had little stomach for a fight and a whole day went by in manœuvring for position. Bothwell offered to fight in single combat, and the Laird of Tullibardine took up his challenge, but the Queen rejected the offer on the grounds that he was not of sufficient rank to fight Bothwell, the Duke of Orkney. She tried in-effectually to make terms for Bothwell, but the lords stood firm. They were determined to die, they said, or take Bothwell prisoner. On hearing this, Bothwell mounted his horse and with a small following rode off in the

direction of Dunbar. Some accounts say that it was because of the Queen's entreaties that he left the field, just as Antony gave up the fight after Cleopatra's pleas; others that the lords allowed him to escape because many of them were implicated with Bothwell in Darnley's murder.

The Queen was then taken prisoner and brought back to Edinburgh. She never saw Bothwell again.

Contemporaries of Mary's return to her capital paint a terrifying chronicle of complete physical and mental collapse. She was put in the house of the Provost of Edinburgh.

> At one o'clock the next morning her Majesty appeared at the window making piteous lamentation, and cried forth to the people that she was held in prison and kept by her own subjects who had betrayed her. She came to the said window in so miserable a state, her hair hanging about her ears, and her breast, yea the most part of her body from the waist up bare and discovered, that no man could look upon her but she moved him to pity and compassion.

The French Ambassador tried to see her but was refused permission. The Scots lords were wary and gave as their excuse for refusal that she could use foreign languages; they were taking no chances with their royal captive. In the evening the Queen was marched to Holyrood Abbey with two hundred men in front, carrying the banner with the dead King on it;

the lords followed with a thousand men. She was hustled away secretly by night to Lochleven, because in Edinburgh the fickle populace was on the rampage, shouting such slogans as: 'Burn her, burn the whore!'

Once arrived at Lochleven, Mary sank into apathy and remained for over two weeks without eating, drinking, or speaking, 'so that many thought she would have died'. The warden of Lochleven Castle was the Earl of Moray's mother, the former mistress of Mary's father. The wheel of Stuart fortunes had turned again to defeat. But the Queen's collapse was temporary; with the gradual return of her spirits, she clearly exerted her ever-useful charm. Lord Ruthven, the son of the murderer of Riccio, fell so much under her spell that he had to be sent away. Mary herself alleged that he had offered her freedom in exchange for her virtue, an allegation which doubtless did him little good.

The lords took no chances with their prisoner and kept her closely guarded, and yet, in spite of their pressures, and her close confinement, she steadfastly refused to abandon Bothwell, saying that 'she would leave her kingdom and dignity to live as a simple damsel with him'. It is possible that such reports came from tainted sources, for the lords were afraid of showing weakness towards the Queen on account of the attitude of the mob. The men no less than the women were incensed against her and now as thoroughly aroused by their preachers against the so-called whore of Scotland as against the whore of Rome.

Although the Queen was in the power of the rebel lords, she had become a problem. They had a trump card, yet they did not know how to play it to their best advantage. Some wished to kill her out of hand as this seemed the simplest solution, but others were already planning new marriages for her. Lord Arbroath and the brother of the Earl of Argyll were two suggestions.

As might be supposed, the Earl of Moray, Mary's brother, was still abroad. He was biding his time, prudent as always. And both the King of France and Queen Elizabeth were anxious to become guardians of the infant Prince, showing how solicitous people can become about the fate of children when inheritances are attached to them.

The imprisoned Mary eventually appeared to have become resigned to her fate, and was reported as being calm, eating meat, dancing, and playing cards. She was even reported to have become fat. This was not surprising as she was pregnant by Bothwell.

It is unlikely that she was as resigned as she seemed. Her courage had returned and there were reports that she had attempted to escape in a small boat alone. As a result she was imprisoned in the tower, the strongest place in the Castle. Nothing daunted, she immediately set about complaining of her treatment, and offered suggestions for her greater comfort. They could treat her, not as a sovereign, but as her father's daughter. She would retire to a nunnery in France. And for good measure, she demanded her son, another gentlewoman to wait on her, an embroiderer to draw for her, a *valet de chambre*, and a minister.

Throckmorton made an attempt to see her, but was refused by the lords. It was then she gave her real reason for refusing to abandon Bothwell, sending a message to Throckmorton to say that if she did this it would be to acknowledge her coming child as a bastard, as she took herself to be 'seven weeks gone with child'.

To add to Mary's misfortune and danger, Knox had now reappeared in Edinburgh, and was preaching about Jezebel, vengeance, and the general destruction of whores. Throckmorton tried to persuade both Knox and Craig to dampen down their exhortations, but added sadly: 'I find them both very austere, furnished with many arguments, some forth of the Scripture.' There was no hope to be found in that quarter, and the Englishman was convinced that the lords had it in their mind to kill her.

By the end of July 1568, the lords had forced Mary to abdicate in favour of her son James. Nau, her secretary, says that she was in bed as a result of a miscarriage of twins when they forced her to sign this abdication. The charges brought against her were 'tyranny, incontinency, as well with Bothwell as with others, having as they say sufficient proof against her for this crime', as well as 'the murder of her husband, by the testimony of her own handwriting'. It is possible that these alleged proofs were the Casket Letters, but Throckmorton said that had she not signed, the lords had forthright plans for her, such as throwing her into the lake, or keeping her in perpetual captivity in some remote island in the ocean.

The abdication signed, the infant King was crowned, a thousand bonfires blazed in Edinburgh, the Castle let off twenty pieces of artillery, and Mr Knox preached a moving sermon on the text that Joas was crowned when very young.

In August, Moray was back in Scotland. The subsequent interview between brother and sister was spread over two days. Throckmorton reported that Moray 'behaved himself rather like a ghostly father to her than a counsellor'. She wept, she acknowledged her faults, she excused her behaviour, and in the end she begged her brother to take over the reins of government. The Earl also took into his safe keeping Mary's jewels, subsequently sending the Scottish Queen's ropes of black pearls to Elizabeth.

It was only seven years since Mary had arrived back in Scotland and Moray was at the helm again. Temporarily the Queen was a spent force even to her compatriots in France. 'The French do not take greatly to heart how this Queen speeds, whether she lives, or dies,' one writer commented.

While Mary lay captive, Bothwell was still at large. The lords had sent various accommodating messages to Queen Elizabeth about him, enquiring whether she would like him killed or 'delivered to your Majesty'. But the English envoy took the practical view that as Bothwell was accompanied by a number of 'desperate persons' there was no great facility for the apprehension of the said Earl. He was not captured, and eventually retreated to the Orkneys, with five ships and several hundred men.

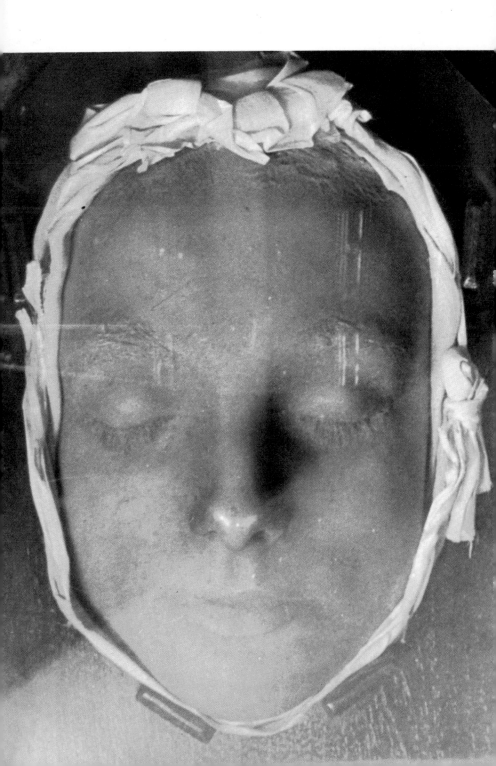

Death mask from Lennoxlove, East Lothian (Trans-Globe).

It was reported that he was intending to use the sea as a refuge and would 'attract the pirates of all countries to him'. Kirkcaldy was then sent to capture the Earl, but his ship struck a rock, and Bothwell disappeared in the direction of Norway where he arrived at Bergen. Here the errant Earl found his former Norwegian wife waiting for him, and was forced into giving her both an annuity and a small ship. It could be said that after many a long year Anne Thorssen's ship had come in, even if Bothwell's had not.

By the end of September, the imprisoned Mary, ever resilient, had won over George Douglas, Moray's half brother. She was even favouring him as one of her suitors, but Moray vetoed the idea. Knowing Mary's pride, he gave as his reason that it was 'overmean a marriage'. The lords were also against it, giving as their view 'because she is young and may have many children which is the thing they would be rid of'. Her marriages had caused them a number of inconveniences, and they preferred to keep the reins in their masculine hands. If there was to be treachery, it was to be male treachery.

This remarkable if erratic Queen then made another attempt to escape, dressed as a laundress, but was discovered by reason of her 'white hands' and promptly rowed back to Lochleven again. Through George Douglas, who was reported to be 'in a fantasy of love' with the imprisoned Queen, she managed to get letters through to her relations abroad, demanding to be rescued by force, and requesting that her letters be burned, 'for should it be known that I have written it may cost a great many lives'. Nearly twenty years later Mary was still putting other people's lives in peril for the sake of her own freedom.

In the event, the letters to the Continent proved unnecessary, for her third attempt at escape from Lochleven was successful. Although George Douglas had been banished from the island, various sympathizers and disgruntled lords were themselves planning her escape, and some of these must have been inside the Castle. On the 2 May 1568, the keys were stolen at suppertime, Mary was taken to a boat, the Castle gates were locked against the gaolers, and the horses stolen. She was met by Lord Seton with a company of horsemen, and was soon in the stronghold of her Hamilton sympathizers, ready to give battle to her bastard brother. She is supposed to have issued a proclamation against Moray calling him, amongst other things, 'a bastard gotten in shameful adultery', and his followers, 'hell hounds, unworthy traitors, and common murderers whom not even the barbarous Turk could pardon or spare'. Like many documents concerned with this Queen, it is said to be a forgery, but the words have the ring of the escaped prisoner bent on revenge.

Within a week the clans had rallied to her standard, and when the day of battle dawned at Langside, on the 15 May, her forces were even larger than the Regent Moray's. The Queen watched the battle from a hill. Although the fighting was hard, 'and more than six score had fallen', the battle was lost. The Queen, seeing her forces defeated, lost her courage, which she so rarely did, and fled, riding more than ninety miles, or so she claimed, until she reached Dundrennan, where she sent an urgent letter to Elizabeth requesting her help.

Mary's friends implored her not to cross into England. Over the centuries the frantic debate between the defeated Queen and her handful of followers still echoes. She refused, she said, to go into France, as an exile or a fugitive, where she had formerly 'appeared in so much glory and splendour'. The wedding in Notre Dame, the triumphal entry into Orléans, the adulation during her growing years, were still pictures in her mind. She would not go back, she would rely on Elizabeth, and on her own claims to the English throne. She had lived nearly fifteen years in France, her active life in Scotland had lasted less than seven, yet nearly twenty years of imprisonment lay in front of her.

On the 16 May, the small party of fugitives crossed the Solway into Cumberland and landed at Workington. Pride had made a fatal decision, the bird had flown into a snare.

28. *The Victorian view of Mary, Queen of Scots escaping from Lochleven Castle* (Mansell Collection)

Chapter XIII

29. *Queen Elizabeth I* (Scottish National Portrait Gallery)

During Mary's imprisonment at Lochleven Elizabeth had written her letters of advice and encouragement, letters which were perhaps over-fulsome in deploring the Scottish Queen's situation. Elizabeth's reason for writing in this vein was her firm belief in the Divine Right of Queens. It was a very different state of affairs to have the same Queen arriving on her soil, demanding asylum and help. As was her wont, Elizabeth pre-varicated, saying that there was nothing she would like better than to re-ceive Mary, but first she must be cleared of the crimes which had been alleged against her.

Sir Francis Knollys had to take this reply to Mary. An air of resignation hangs about his letters, for he says the Queen 'fell into her ordinary in-veighing against my Lord of Moray'. The Scots Queen was demanding a free passage through England to solicit aid from her foreign relatives, and when she found Elizabeth would not receive her, fell into 'great passion and weeping'. But in spite of the tears Elizabeth remained pleasantly adamant.

Mary wrote bitterly to her uncle, the Cardinal of Lorraine: 'I have en-dured injuries, calumnies, imprisonment, famine, cold, heat, flight not knowing whither, ninety-two miles across the country without stopping or alighting, and then I have had to sleep upon the ground, and drink sour milk, and eat oatmeal without bread, and have been three nights like the owls, without a female in this country, where to crown all, I am little else than a prisoner.' She had come a long way from the Court at St Germain-en-Laye.

Yet in spite of her overwhelming defeats the Queen remained un-daunted. Even Knollys was impressed by her.

This lady and Princess is a notable woman. She seemeth to regard no ceremoni-ous honour beside the acknowledging of her estate regal. She showeth a disposition to speak much, to be bold, to be pleasant, and to be very familiar. She showeth a great desire to be avenged of her enemies, the thing she most thirsteth after is victory, so that for victory's sake, pain and perils seem pleasant unto her.

Two instincts came to Mary from her French blood and upbringing, a thirst for *la Gloire*, and panache, that compound of courage and pride. But she had fallen into the hands of a woman who had learned the best lessons of princes, patience, and an ability to choose, and listen to, subtle advisers. She was not going to allow Mary to become a rallying point for her Catholic subjects, or a lever for the ambitions of either France or Spain.

From May 1568, when Mary crossed the border into England, until February 1587, when she was executed, the war was waged between the rash, courageous, but imprisoned Queen and the patient circumlocutory Elizabeth moving freely in her glittering Court. It was an underground war set against the background of the ambitions of the French and Spanish Kings, the religious wars in France, the internecine strife in Scotland, and the destruction of the Old Religion in England. If Queen Victoria remarked that Queen Elizabeth was cruel to her ancestress, the Queen of Scots, the remark was made against the background of a stable state. Queen Elizabeth operated in a small country beset by enemies on two fronts, undermined by religious feuds, and was always in fear of plots against her life. Mary was to prove a rallying point for these.

The imprisoned always attract sympathy. In Carlisle, Mary was 'in a small dark room with a barred window'. Yet when de Montmorin visited her there, she immediately sent out letters, with his connivance, asking for military help from France, and requesting aid from the Spanish Ambassador in London.

Elizabeth's advisers, who supported the Regent Moray, and whose policy was the stabilization of Scotland and the eventual unity of the two countries, regarded Mary as a stumbling block to that stability. Given the smallest encouragement she would be springing to horse, and fostering new rebellions.

After his various interviews with Mary, Knollys wrote to Cecil: 'The safest and most direct policy would be to aid the Regent in time, and if the spots in Queen Mary's coat could be made manifest the sooner it were done the better.' But Elizabeth always acted later rather than sooner.

Then began the long, melancholy odyssey of Mary's various prisons, and the equally long series of letters penned by Mary's bold hand. There were demands to be set free, complaints of her treatment, reproaches, menaces, references to her powerful relations abroad; letters demanding to see Elizabeth in person, to be allowed to put her own case, to request permission to see her son, and letters full of charm: 'My dear sister, do not act like the serpent and block your ears, because I am not an enchanter but your sister and natural cousin.' But to all the threats, entreaties, and complaints Elizabeth remained deaf. If she was a serpent, she was a serpent with a sharp tongue and an acute intelligence.

From Carlisle, which was judged to be too near the Scottish border for England's comfort, Mary was moved to Bolton, and in the autumn of 1568 investigations were begun into the question of Mary's guilt or innocence in the matter of Darnley's murder. This quasi-trial put Elizabeth into a position where she might have to make a decision, a stance she always sought to avoid. She told the Spanish Ambassador that if Mary were found innocent it would be bad for England's interests, and if guilty that also could bring difficulties in its train. There were two investigations, during which the Casket Letters were produced, but the judgement was left in abeyance, for some of the instigators of Darnley's murder were still in power in Scotland.

An attempt was made to get Mary again to abdicate, but once more the stone wall of her pride, courage, and obstinacy became apparent. Her former abdication was under duress, this time she was not giving way. 'The last word I will say in my life will be as Queen of Scotland. If I yield it will be said, it was by fear of being publicly accused, and fearing I had no good cause, and I preferred not to yield to avoid a condemnation.'

At the time of the rising of the northern Catholic lords, it was deemed judicious to move the Scots Queen to a safer prison. This was carried out, but not without difficulties—in fact it was even mooted that, so little did she approve of the move, she might have to be forcibly lifted from her bed and carried off in a litter. In spite of her complaints, she was transferred to Tutbury, under the care of the Earl of Shrewsbury, and his wife, the tough Bess of Hardwick.

From then on, the Regent Moray appeared to have a firmer grip on Scotland, and Elizabeth certainly had a firmer grip on her cousin. Less than eighteen months later, the Regent was shot by James Hamilton of Bothwellhaugh. In spite of Mary's former protestations of affection for her brother, or the fact that she immediately wore the deepest mourning for him, she made certain that a pension should be paid to the escaped assassin. Words were one thing, and actions another, and she had not forgiven Moray for the investigations conducted into her conduct by Elizabeth, any more than she had in the past forgiven Darnley for his part in the murder of Riccio.

But the imprisoned Queen had still lost neither her courage, her hopes, nor her ability to put the lives of others in jeopardy, and in 1571 a new plot was mounted. Amongst other machinations the conspiracy included the invasion of England by the Spanish, the killing of Queen Elizabeth, and inevitably, marriage for Mary with the Duke of Norfolk. The intricate threads of this plot, engineered by Ridolfi, a banker, led from Spain to France and back to London, and included dissident Catholics, now more than ever subjected to physical and financial restrictions for upholding their faith. Her charm and her position as upholder of the Old Faith were two of the assets she was to use to the end of her life.

While encouraging Elizabeth's subjects to rebel, she was also negotiating with the Pope for her divorce from Bothwell. Her grounds were that she had been forced into the marriage, and now wished for an annulment. Bothwell himself was rotting in a Danish prison, where he died mad. It was hard for a man of action, a pirate in spirit, to be deprived of freedom. He did not survive the restrictions as well as his more resilient spouse.

In spite of the ciphers and the secrecy, the agents, the scuttling to and fro, the Ridolfi plot was discovered. The end-product of the intrigues, the hopes, the fears, and the treacheries was that the Duke of Norfolk was sent to the Tower. On the 2 June 1572 he was executed. Elizabeth hesitated about signing his death warrant, always aware of her own mother's death on the scaffold; she hated and feared the act of bringing death to others. Against the advice of her counsellors, she spared Mary's life.

But the knowledge of foreign plots caused the persecution and torturings of the English Catholics to grow apace. Jesuits whose sole purpose was to keep the Faith alive were racked, hanged, drawn, and quartered as Spanish spies. Meanwhile the Queen of Scots settled down to a long imprisonment enlivened by the vast political correspondence which she kept up with foreign Courts and her foreign relatives. It was comparatively easy for her to get letters through from her various prisons, for she was not closely guarded and still kept the semblance of a Court around her. Indeed the modern term house detention rather than imprisonment might in some ways be a better description of her circumstances. Servants took out letters in the heels of their shoes, handkerchiefs were impregnated with messages written in invisible ink. Baskets of provisions, taken for charitable purposes to needy villagers, had false bottoms in which were hidden letters destined for overseas.

By 1585, Cecil, and his spymaster Walsingham, had decided that the situation had continued for too long. Mary was a potential danger, she had too many spies abroad, and in view of the political situation with Spain, she was removed to a closer confinement at Tutbury in the charge of Sir Amyas Paulet, a strict Puritan. It is said that this was carried out so that Mary would chafe under her tighter restriction, and that, on this account, she would fall an easy prey to temptations to open up a new seditious correspondence with the outside world. Other historians say that Walsingham did not set a trap for the Queen but was merely following his craft of obtaining reliable political information and that the discovery of the Babington plot was a happy bonus. On balance, it seems probable that a trap was indeed being prepared.

Anthony Babington, the chief instigator of this plot, had been page to Queen Mary when she was imprisoned at Sheffield, and had fallen under her spell. He was marked out by Mary's agents abroad as a fitting leader of a Catholic insurrection, and in 1586 induced to play the leading part in the conspiracy which aimed at the murder of Elizabeth and the release of Mary. The conspirators were rash and Walsingham heard of the plot.

But moated Tutbury was too closely guarded for Walsingham's provocateur plans, and Mary was moved, again not without difficulties, to

Chartley Manor. Moving a Queen was not a small operation, even if it were only a question of twelve miles, and Sir Amyas was not in favour of it. 'You would hardly believe the baggage that this Queen and her company have of books, apparel, and other like trash. Nau and Curle [her secretaries] praying me to make provision of 80 carts at least, and yet they have no bedding, nor other household stuff save the Queen's wardrobe, a matter of nothing.'

At Chartley, the plot was set in train. Messages were concealed in a barrel of ale. The brewer, a good man of business, was paid both by Walsingham, and by Mary, and in addition demanded a higher price for the beer, for the trouble he was put to in the matter. Starting with a simple message in a barrel of beer from Burton-on-Trent the web of the Babington plot spread to the Low Countries, to Spain, and through to the Vatican. Philip II awaited the rising of the English Catholics and the killing of Elizabeth to invade England, though many of the Catholics involved had no knowledge that Queen Elizabeth's life was at risk; they imagined they were merely supporting the Queen of Scots' rights of succession to the throne. Only the leaders of the plot knew the truth.

It can be said that to trap an imprisoned woman in this way was treachery of the blackest kind. It seemed certain that the restrictions on Mary's liberty would lead her on to some rash act, and they did. But much treachery was in her own nature, in her relationship with Elizabeth, and her ambitious, proud, and unyielding character helped to enmesh her.

The end came quickly. Walsingham was in possession of the facts. Careful copies had been taken of all the letters which Mary had sent. The conspirators were betrayed, hunted down, and arrested. Even Babington tried to turn Queen's evidence. But still Walsingham wanted absolute proofs. He needed Mary's correspondence and, still more important, the ciphers. She must be incriminated up to the hilt. The news of the discovery and betrayal of the plot was kept from her. No message could be sent through to her without the prior knowledge of Sir Amyas Paulet.

Like many a spymaster before, and since, Walsingham used his knowledge of the Queen's character and tastes to separate her from the precious and incriminating correspondence. She had never lost her love of outdoor sports, and chafed under house arrest. Uplifted by the progress of the plot she had written: 'God hath not set me so low but that I am able to handle my crossbow for killing a deer, and to gallop after the hounds on horseback.'

Sir Amyas suggested that a buck should be killed in a park some distance from Chartley. In good mood at the prospect of her coming deliverance, the Queen agreed. It is impossible not to contemplate without melancholy the picture of the captive Queen with her false hopes setting out for a morning's carefree hunting. The party which set off on that brisk morning included Mary's two secretaries. But as soon as they reached the Park, the Queen's party was stopped by a number of horsemen.

Perhaps at the sight of the horsemen she imagined that deliverance had come at last after eighteen years. If so she was brutally undeceived.

Sir Thomas Gorges rode towards the Queen's party and presented his orders for the arrest of Mary's secretaries, and the truth came with the shock of hopes destroyed. Mary raged and demanded that her servants should cut down the men. But it was too late for action, too late for courage, her servants were disarmed and she herself was led off to a new place of imprisonment at Tixall.

Sir Amyas took possession of her correspondence, notebooks, and letters from fellow conspirators in England and abroad, the fruits of many days and nights of coding and de-coding. The haul included sixty ciphers. She was not a woman who was inclined to do anything in a small way.

Now, as after the battle of Carberry Hill, her morale briefly crumbled, and when she was brought back to Chartley two weeks later she was ill and dishevelled. But she soon recovered her courage and her kindliness towards others. One of her ladies had been delivered of a premature child, and as she was forbidden a priest the Queen baptized the child herself.

When she discovered the ransacking of her papers, she said, 'Some of you will be sorry for this!' and the brunt of her anger fell on her gaoler. Sir Amyas, weary of tears, reproaches, and anger, tried to get Elizabeth to remove Mary to the Tower, without result. Elizabeth wrote asking God to reward him 'for thy most troublesome charge so well discharged', but to Mary she showed a different face. 'Let repentance take place, and let not the fiend possess her, so as her better part may be lost.'

The papers were examined in detail, and trial was decided upon. Peers and judges were convened. The judging of the Queen took place at Fotheringay Castle in a great chamber sixty feet long. Between rows of the greatest in the realm, Mary entered in a plain grey dress, and took her seat in the centre of the room. She had refused to admit her guilt to Elizabeth or confess her fault. Conscious of her status as Queen, and her ability to debate, she was prepared to face and answer her accusers.

Her replies were ingenious. As a Queen she was not answerable to the laws of the land, she was not a subject of Queen Elizabeth, she was a fellow sovereign. She knew nothing of Anthony Babington; even when his letters were read to her, she challenged her accusers to prove she had received them. When her own letter to Babington in cipher was produced, she denied that it was hers. If her ciphers had been used they could have been counterfeited. She had been held unjustly prisoner for many years, and as a Princess she was not answerable to any tribunal. Her Divine Right still held.

The enquiry took two days. William Cecil wrote: 'The Queen of the castle was content to appear again before us. Her intention was to move to pity by artificial speeches, and to lay the blame on the Queen and the Council that all past troubles did ensue . . . whereby great debate fell yesternight very long, and this day renewed with great stomaching.'

Mary remained staunch in her denials and the enquiry was moved to London, and finally to Parliament. The knights and burgesses were not firm on the Divine Right of Kings and Queens. Both Lords and Commons were decided in their view. 'The Queen of Scots regarded the Crown of England as belonging to herself. She was hardened in malice and so bent on the destruction of her Majesty. From the day the Queen of Scots came to England she has been a canker at its heart corrupting the minds of the people.' They demanded an execution.

Queen Elizabeth, however, hesitated. To execute a Queen was not a small or insignificant action. Diplomatically it held risks. The French were busy trying to save Mary, for she was Queen Dowager of France. Even King James of Scotland was roused into some semblance of activity, although his anxious thoughts were bent more towards the securing of his succession to the English throne rather than on the rescue of his mother.

Mary was now solemnly warned that if she did not confess the sentence would be carried out. She refused, saying that she would sacrifice her life for her Faith. Politely she was told that this was not the reason she was to die, the death sentence was demanded for the plot to murder her fellow Queen. Again she denied it, and when Sir Amyas Paulet removed the hangings with her queenly insignia from the wall, she hung a crucifix in their place. If Elizabeth was going to execute her, she was going to die ostensibly as a martyr for her Faith.

When the final message of death was conveyed to her she is variously

reported as having received it with great perturbation and with great calm. To the end, the conflicting sides of her character washed backwards and forwards across her contemporaries as they have done with chroniclers ever since.

On the day of her execution she passed through the ranks of hundreds of gentlemen assembled to witness it. The scaffold was covered with a black cloth, and she mounted it with an impassive face. When a Protestant cleric attempted to speak to her, she broke in, saying that she was a Catholic and would die a Catholic.

The Dean, Dr Fletcher, attempted to get her to confess her sins and be converted to Protestantism, but she knelt and prayed in Latin.

Her black robes were removed by the executioner. 'Her petticoat was of red velvet, her bodice of scarlet satin, and having been disrobed of her petticoat, one of her ladies brought to her a pair of scarlet satin sleeves in which she put her arms, and thus she was executed all in scarlet.' A scarlet victim on a black scaffold. She knelt down murmuring, 'Into thy hands, O Lord, I commend my spirit'. The executioner made a false blow, only grazing her neck, but the second blow severed her head.

> So the executioner cut off her head, saving one little gristle, which being cut asunder he lifted up her head to the view of all the assembly and bade God Save the Queen. Then, her dress of lawn falling from off her head, it appeared as grey as one of threescore and ten years old, polled very short . . . her lips stirred up and down a quarter of an hour after her head was cut off. Then one of the executioners, pulling off her garters, espied her little dog which was crept under her clothes, which could not be gotten forth but by force, yet afterward would not depart from the dead corpse, but came and lay between her head and her shoulders, which being imbrued with her blood was carried away and washed.

The bells rang in London and bonfires blazed across the country for the deliverance, while Elizabeth wept for the bloody death of her cousin, and raged at her Council for executing the Queen of Scots without her final consent.

Mary Stuart's death was the signal for a change of heart in Paris. She had after all, it now seemed, died a martyr for her Faith, and was a symbol of the perfidy of Albion. The following year Spain, freed from the fear of France by the Queen's death, launched the Armada for which Mary had always hoped.

Now nearly four hundred years later her life and character remain a question mark, in that so many of her actions appear in conflict with her words. Nostradamus, the astrologer, told Catherine de Médicis that when he looked at the child, Mary Stuart, he saw blood. If he saw the blood of Mary, perhaps he also saw the blood of the men who were destroyed in her cause. As a lodestar she had drawn men to her, as a catalyst she had attracted plots and counter-plots. Though she died bravely, as a Queen, she died in the end a Queen of disorder and violence.

Her contemporaries saw her as a saint or a devil. Since then the views have fluctuated; the romantic revival depicted a tragic victim, the Victorians a menace to the truth of Protestantism, the Catholics a witness to the Old Religion. French writers show her as a true woman full of the faults, the follies, and the glory of womanhood, modern writers as a female destructive and destroying for Freudian lust. Perhaps each generation sees in her some microcosm of itself.

Her faults were balanced by her virtues. The fantastic physical fortitude, *élan*, and power of initiative she inherited from her Scottish ancestors were set against a lack of prudence incompatible with those virtues. Her upbringing in France utterly unfitted her to rule her fractious, turbulent Scottish subjects. The 'lenity and dulciness' always feared by John Knox did indeed bring this Queen to fearful destruction.

She will remain to the end of time a proud, courageous enigma.

32. *Mary Stuart canonized* (Mansell Collection)

MARIA SCOTIÆ ET GALLIÆ DE FACTO, DE IVRE ANGLIÆ ET HYBERNIÆ REGINA, a suis deturbata, in Angliam refugij causa descendens, cognatæ Elizabethæ tum regnantis perfidia, Senatusqz Anglici inuidia, post 19. captiuitatis annos religionis ergo capite obtruncata martyrium consummauit. Anno Ætatis Regnæqz 45 A° 1587.

Summary of Events

1542: 8 Dec.: Mary Stuart is born at Linlithgow Castle

14 Dec.: James V dies and she succeeds to the throne of Scotland

1543: 23 July: Taken to Stirling Castle by Cardinal Beaton

1547: 8 Feb.: Henry VIII dies

9 Sept.: Infant Queen crowned at Stirling

10 Sept.: Battle of Pinkie Cleugh, the Queen taken to Inchmahome Abbey on the Lake of Menteith

1548: 7 July: The Estates ratify agreement of Mary's marriage to the Dauphin of France

7 Aug.: Mary Stuart sent to France

13 Aug.: Arrival at Roscoff in Britanny

11 Oct.: Arrival at the French Court of Henri II at St Germain-en-Laye

1554: 1 Jan.: Gives discourse in Latin at the French Court

1558: 4 April: Signs deeds about the Scottish succession

19 April: Fiançailles of Mary Stuart and François the Dauphin

24 April: They are married at Notre Dame in Paris

17 Nov.: Mary Tudor dies and Elizabeth succeeds to the throne of England

1559: 10 July: Henri II is killed jousting and François II, husband of Mary Stuart, succeeds to the throne

1560: 10 Jan.: Marie de Guise, Queen Regent of Scotland, dies

March: The Conjuration (Conspiracy) of Amboise

6 July: Treaty of Edinburgh is signed

6 Dec.: François II dies of an ear infection and Catherine de Médicis becomes Queen Regent of France

1561: 10 Aug.: Mary Stuart arrives at Calais and sets sail for Scotland on the 15 August

19 Aug.: Arrival at Leith

1562: Autumn: The Queen rides north against the Earl of Huntly accompanied by her brother the Earl of Moray

1563: Feb.: Chastelard executed

1565: Jan.: Lord Darnley goes to Scotland

29 July: Marriage with Henry, Earl of Darnley

25 Aug.: Mary with Darnley takes the field against the rebel Lords

10 Oct.: Moray leaves for England

1566: Jan.: Plot hatched against Riccio by the Scottish Lords

9 March: Riccio murdered in Holyrood Palace

18 March: Mary re-enters Edinburgh

19 June: James VI born

17 Dec.: Baptism of James VI at Stirling Castle

1567: 9 Feb.: Murder of Darnley

12 April: James Hepburn, Earl of Bothwell, indicted for murder, and acquitted

3 May: Bothwell divorced from Jean Gordon, sister of the Earl of Huntly

15 May: Marriage of Mary and Bothwell

15 June: Defeat of Mary and Bothwell at Carberry Hill

1567: 17 June: Mary brought back to Edinburgh and imprisoned at Lochleven

24 July: Signs abdication, and Moray named as Regent

1568: 2 May: Escape from Lochleven

13 May: Battle of Langside

16 May: Crosses Solway into England. Imprisoned by Elizabeth

1569: 26 Feb.: Mary is removed to Tutbury under the Earl of Shrewsbury

23 Jan.: Moray assassinated

1570: Mary divorced from Bothwell

1572: 2 June: Duke of Norfolk executed

1585: April: Mary is transferred to Tutbury under Sir Amyas Paulet

1586: Aug.: Arrest at Tixall

25 Sept.: Transferred to Fotheringay

1587: 8 Feb.: Mary executed at Fotheringay

1 Aug.: Buried at Peterborough

1588: April–Oct.: The Armada sails and is defeated

1603: James VI succeeds to the throne of England as James I

33. *Mary's death warrant signed by Elizabeth* (British Museum)

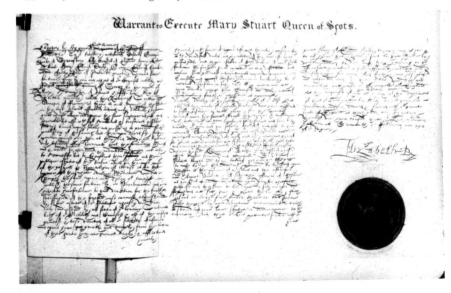

A Select Bibliography

The Queens and the Hive. Edith Sitwell
The England of Elizabeth. A. L. Rowse
Elizabethans at Home. E. Burton and F. Kelly
Elizabeth the Great. Elizabeth Jenkins
The Other Face. Philip Caraman
Henry VIII. John Bowle
James I. Mathew
Bad Queen Bess. Piers Compton
John Gerard. Caraman
Les Amours. Ronsard
Elizabeth and Essex. Strachey
Elizabeth and Mary Stuart. Frank Mumby
Fall of Mary Stuart. Frank Mumby
The Four Maries. Arnold Fleming
Marie Stuart. Filon (Paris)
Marie Stuart. Zweig (Paris)
Histoire de Marie Stuart. Jules Gauthier (2 vols.)
La Conjuration d'Amboise. Lucien Romier
Le Cardinal de Lorraine. Guillemin (1847)
La Conjuration d'Amboise et de Genève. Henri Naef
Les Débuts des Guerres de Religion—Catherine de Médicis (Entre Guise et Conde). Bernard
    de Lacombe
The Brood of False Lorraine. H. Noel Williams
Marie Stuart, son procès et son exécution. M. de Chantelauze
Massacre of St Bartholomew. Henry Noguerre
Case of Mary Queen of Scots and Elizabeth Queen of England. Hugh Campbell
History of England. Froude
Mystery of Mary Stuart. Andrew Lang
Tyrannous Reign of Mary Stewart. George Buchanan's account. Tr. W. A. Gatherer
Casket Letters. Henderson
Examination of the Letters of Mary Queen of Scots. Walter Gooddall
History of the Reformation. John Knox
The Thundering Scot. Geddes MacGregor
The Penicuik Jewels of Mary Queen of Scots. Walter Seton
Defeat of the Spanish Armada. Garrett Mattingley

Porphyria—a Royal Malady. British Medical Association
The Scotland of Queen Mary and the Religious Wars. Agnes Mure Mackenzie
Brief Lives. John Aubrey
Crime of Mary Stuart. George Malcolm Thomson
Conflicts in Tudor and Stuart England (History Today)
Mary Queen of Scots in Captivity. J. D. Leader